Tables of diseases and signs of the zodiac, and diseases and planets
(see pp. 79-82). Biblioteca de Catalunya 634, fols 89v-90r
(reproduced with permission).

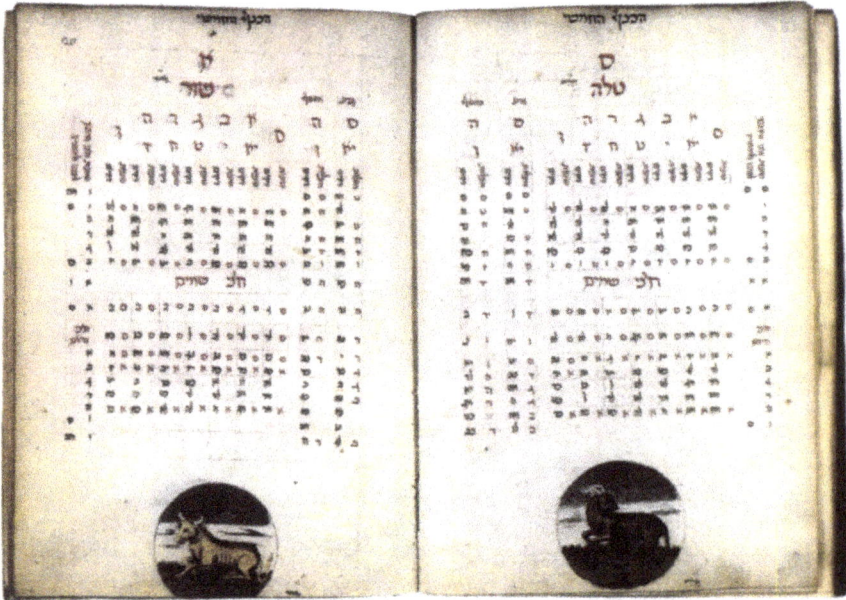

MS Paris, BN héb. 1077: Six Wings of Immanuel Bonfils, and other astronomical and calendrical texts. Germany, c. 1475-1490, parchment (except for 3 paper leaves)

Immanuel Ben Jacob Bonfils is foremost known for the astronomical tables which he drew up in the year 1365 in the city of Tarascon which he called "Shesh Kenafayim" (Six Wings; cf. Is. 6:2). The work was translated into Latin in 1406 and into Byzantine Greek in 1435. These tables are preserved in many manuscript copies. Each "wing" contains a number of astronomical tables concerning the movements of the sun and the moon for determining the times and magnitudes of solar and lunar eclipses as well as the day of the new moon. The tables themselves are largely based on the tables of the ninth-century Arab astronomer al-Battani, as the author acknowledges in the preface. But they are presented according to the Jewish calendar and adapted to the longitude and latitude of Tarascon. These tables were consulted by European scholars as late as the seventeenth century. The fifth "wing" is dedicated to the zodiac. In this German copy from the end of the fifteenth century, folios 19v to 25 have one zodiacal sign on each page. These signs are set in medallions with their Latin names transcribed in Hebrew characters.

Lit.: M. Garel, D'une main forte. Manuscrits hébreux des collections francaises, Paris, 1991, no. 109; Encyclopaedia Judaica, vol. 4, cols. 1207-1208, entry: "Bonfils, Immanuel Ben Jacob" (B.R. Goldstein).

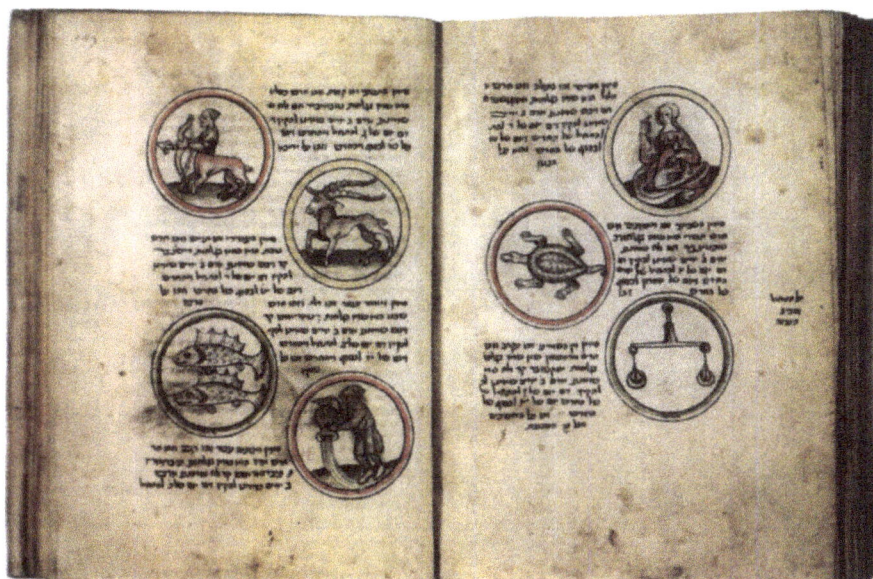

MS Paris, BN héb. 1120: Medical astrology and other texts.
Southern Germany, c. 1480-1500, parchment

This medical miscellany contains treatises by Hippocrates, Galen, Maimonides, and others. At the end of the volume (fols 135-146) we find an un-
titled treatise that deals with the relationship between astrology and medicine,
explains the astral influences, and determines the days proper for bloodletting. The instructions for bloodletting in fols 143v-145 are illuminated with
the signs of the zodiac, which illustrate the purpose of the anonymous author.
The signs of the zodiac in medallion-shaped illustrations are painted in naive
style. The zodiac iconography, characteristic of Ashkenazi prayer books for
the high holidays (Mahzorim) since the thirteenth century, is copied in this
secular manuscript. The style of these medallions recalls the woodcuts of the
almanacs and popular calendars printed and sold in southern Germany at
the end of the fifteenth century, and especially evokes the productions of the
regions around Ulm and Augsburg. Widely distributed, these xylographies
from the beginning of the art of printing left their stamp on the illumination
of later manuscripts.

Lit.: M. Garel, D'une main forte. Manuscrits hébreux des collections francaises,
Paris, 1991, no. 110.

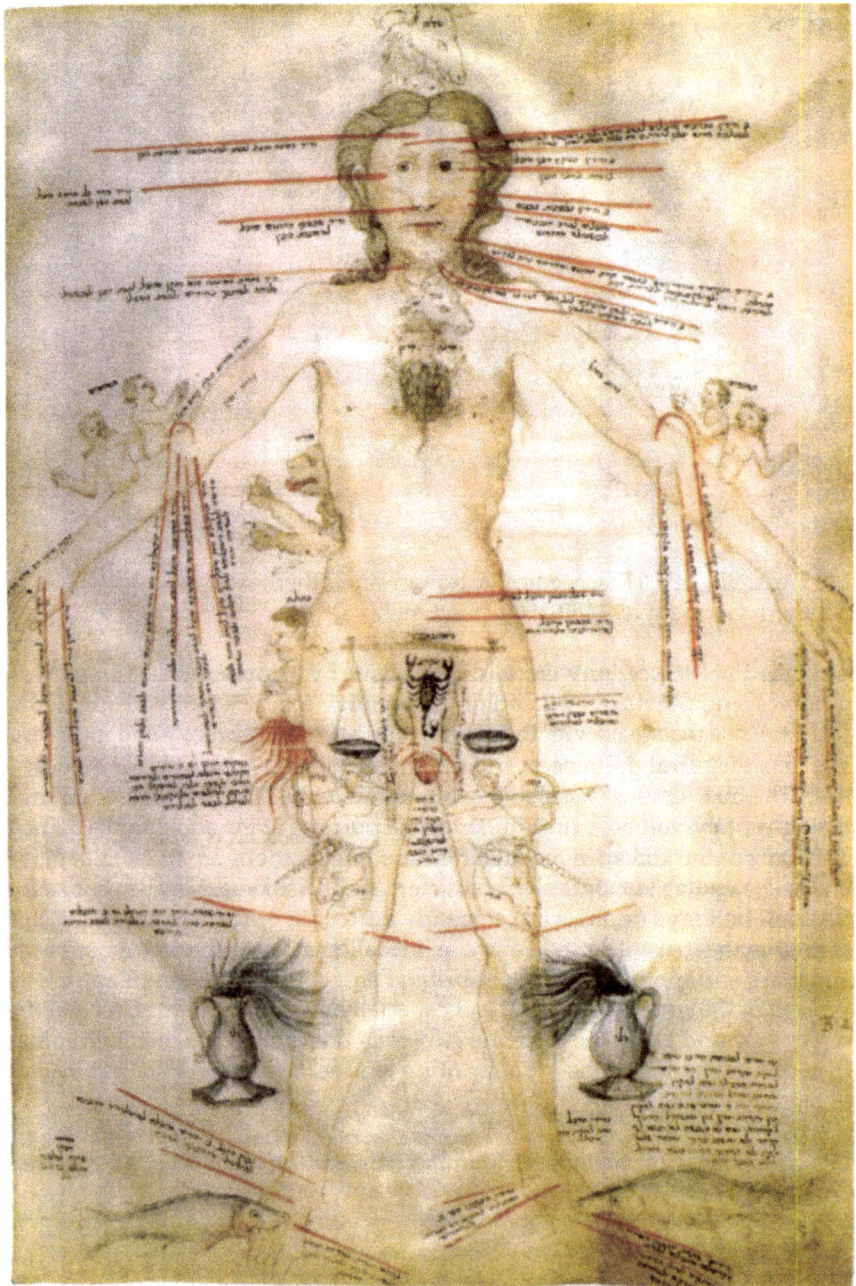

Bloodletting Man

Manuscript from Provence, containing several medical texts, mostly translated fragments of the Medical Treatise of Jean of Damascus, c.1400. 36 x 24 cm.

The only known representation of the homo signorum combined with the homo venarum, where all the positions used for bloodletting are labeled in Hebrew. This illustrates the influence of astrology on the organs and on the choice of the place of bloodletting.

The signs of the zodiac are shown on the parts of the body and limbs they were thought to govern. The absence of any specifically Jewish features in the iconography of the signs of the zodiac indicates that this well-executed figure was copied from a non-Jewish model. Bibliothèque Nationale de France, Paris, Ms. hebr. 1181, folio 264v.

Hebrew Medical Astrology:
David Ben Yom Tov, Kelal Qaṭan

Original Hebrew Text,
Medieval Latin Translation,
Modern English Translation

Hebrew Medical Astrology:
David Ben Yom Tov, Kelal Qaṭan

Original Hebrew Text,
Medieval Latin Translation,
Modern English Translation

Gerrit Bos
Charles Burnett
Tzvi Langermann

American Philosophical Society
Philadelphia • 2005

TRANSACTIONS
of the
AMERICAN PHILOSOPHICAL SOCIETY
Held at Philadelphia
For Promoting Useful Knowledge
Volume 95, Part 5

ISBN-10: 0-87169-955-9
ISBN-13: 978-0-87169-955-8
US ISSN: 0065-9746

Library of Congress Cataloging-in Publication Data

Ben Yom Tov, David, 14th cent.
    [Kelal qaṭan. Polyglot]
    Hebrew medical astrology : David Ben Yom Tov, kelal qatan. Original Hebrew text, medieval Latin translation, modern English translation / [edited by] Gerrit Bos, Charles Burnett, Tzvi Langermann.
        p. cm. — (Transactions of the American Philosophical Society ; v. 95, pt. 5)
        Includes bibliographical references and index.
        ISBN-13: 978-0-87169-955-8 (pbk.)
        1. Medical astrology. I. Bos, Gerrit, 1948– II. Burnett, Charles. III. Langermann, Y. Tzvi. IV. Title. V. Series.

    BF1718.B3712 2005
    133.5'861—dc22

                                                                    2005048119

Contents

Color Plates for Figures 1, 2, 3 and 4 appear in the front of the book

Acknowledgments

It is our great pleasure to offer to the reader this edition of the original Hebrew text, medieval Latin translation and modern English translation of the *Kelal Qaṭan* (*Concise Summary*) composed by David Ben Yom Tov, a Hebrew scholar who lived in the first half of the fourteenth century. This text is the most detailed and extensive original Hebrew treatise on astrological medicine surviving in Hebrew literature. While all three authors have read, criticized, and otherwise contributed to the entire endeavor, Gerrit Bos takes primary responsibility for the Hebrew text and English translation, Tzvi Langermann for the Introduction and Charles Burnett for the Latin text. On this occasion we thank José Chabás for obtaining a copy of the Latin manuscript and for interpreting Catalan words, Benjamin Richler for help with Hebrew manuscripts, and the libraries of Barcelona, Oxford, and Paris for the manuscripts we consulted.

Chapter One

Introduction

We present the reader here with a study of *Kelal Qatan* by David Ben Yom Tov, known in Latin simply as David Iudaeus. This is a text on medical astrology, dealing primarily with the astrological indications pertaining especially to fevers. Our introduction is made up of several parts. We shall first sketch a history of this branch of medical astrology from antiquity up to and including *Sefer ha-Me'orot* (*The Book of the Luminaries*), written by Abraham Ibn Ezra and the most important source for *Kelal Qatan*. Following that, we review the scant existing biographical information concerning David and information about the manuscripts (Hebrew and Latin) used for our edition and give a concise recap of the contents of *Kelal Qatan*. Next we survey all the other medieval Hebrew texts related to medical astrology that have come to our attention. This inspection leads us to conclude that astrology was an interesting feature, but not at all a prominent element, in the corpus of Hebrew and Judaeo-Arabic medical writings. Finally, a short postscript discusses an entirely different tradition in medical astrology, which was also present in Hebrew literature, namely, the supposed correlation between certain asterisms and diseases of the eyes.

Our edition and translation are final products, meeting rigorous academic standards. Similarly, the survey of Hebrew texts in the second part of the introduction is intended to be exhaustive. Not so, however, the conspectus that begins in the next paragraph. In the course of preparing it, we have encountered several highly interesting texts, all of them unpublished and unstudied even in a preliminary fashion. They appear to be of crucial importance for our subject, they warrant independent study, and, in fact, we hope to turn our attention to at least some of them in the future. The picture that begins to emerge from our admittedly hurried study is that a critical reappraisal of the relationship between medicine and astrology took place in that murky suture between the end of classical antiquity and the beginning of Islamic civilization. The reappraisal was critical in both senses of the word: it was of momentous import in directing subsequent developments; and it involved a reassessment of ancient authorities from a stance that was not entirely submissive. We believe that the story that we are about to embark upon is a plausible account in terms of the current state of research; it certainly points to some very promising avenues for future research.

Astrological Medicine: A Historical Sketch

The astrological medicine which forms the core of *Kelal Qaṭ an* and which seems, on the basis of the texts that we have been able to examine, to have been the most significant application of astrology to medicine, consists in correlations between the phases of the moon and the progress of fevers, most particularly, the "crises" or "critical days" that played such an important role in Greek medicine. These are the days on which the fever can be expected to reach a climax, the outcome of which is fateful for the patient. These correlations provide prognoses of the severity of the ailment and the patient's chances of survival, as well as guides to the most efficacious—and the most dangerous—times for therapeutic intervention. Several factors contributed to the theoretical connections thought to obtain between the moon's phases and fevers. First, there is the moon's association with water, or fluids in general, attested to most obviously by the connection between the phases of the moon and the height of ocean tides. Since fevers were thought to result from superfluities of one of the humors, and the humors are liquid, their connection with the moon would seem to follow logically. Second, the moon waxes and wanes, and fevers have their paroxysms and abatements, crises and periods of relative ease. The observation that both the moon and fevers exhibit cyclic behavior seemed to indicate a close connection between the two. Finally, and clearly related to both of the first two factors, there is the theory of critical days that is so important in Greek medicine. Crises were observed, or thought, to occur in cycles of seven days. Though there are other ways to interpret these hebdomads, they do roughly parallel the quarters of the moon.

The first two of these points are made by Ptolemy in his *Tetrabiblos*, one of the foundational texts of ancient and medieval astrology.

Concerning the moon's connection with moisture, he writes, "Most of the moon's power consists of humidifying, clearly because it is close to the earth and because of the moist exhalations therefrom. Its action therefore is precisely this, to soften and cause putrefaction in bodies for the most part, but it shares moderately also in the heating power because of light which it receives from the sun."[1]

With regard to the astrological significance of the moon's cycles Ptolemy observes, "For in its waxing from new moon to first quarter the moon is more productive of moisture; in its passage from first quarter to full, of heat; from full to last quarter, of dryness, and from last quarter to occultation, of cold."[2]

The connection between critical days and the moon's phases was made by some ancient commentators to Hippocrates' *Aphorisms*. In the translation of W.H.S. Jones, *Aphorisms* II.24 states, "The fourth day is indicative of the seven; the eighth is the beginning of another week; the eleventh is to be watched, as being the fourth day of the second week; again the seventeenth is to be watched, being the fourth from the fourteenth and the seventh from the eleventh."[3] Galen does not comment on this passage, but Palladius (sixth century?) does. His commentary is no longer extant in Greek, but it has recently been rediscovered by Hinrich Biesterfeldt and Y. Tzvi Langermann in one Arabic and two Hebrew versions. In his gloss to this aphorism, Palladius remarks that "Hippocrates wishes to inform us that the days of acute diseases follow the same course as the moon's motion on account of the swiftness of the moon's motion. Similarly, illnesses that are prolonged follow the course of the sun, since the sun's motion is slow." Just as prolonged illnesses correspond to the four seasons, so the crises of acute fevers must correspond to the lunar phases.[4]

To be sure, Palladius has noted that the number of days in each part of the cycle is the same for the moon and for acute fevers. He draws no connection here between the moon's phase or position relative to any star and the onset of illness or the purgation administered by the physician. However, it does not seem to require a great leap of thought to connect together all three of our observations and to draw conclusions for both prognosis and therapy from the moon's positions at various stages of the illness.

Galen does take note, however, of the moon's role in his *On Critical Days*, where the connection of the moon's phases, and some planetary aspects as well, with the theory of critical days, takes up the better part of Book Three. Tamsyn Barton, who has been endeavoring to revise the common perception of Galen as someone hostile to astrology, observes that *On Critical Days* "certainly poses a problem for those who would like to excise as spurious those parts of the Galenic corpus that take on board astrology."[5] Yet overall one cannot say that the stars play an important role in Galen's explanations of medical phenomena; for example, there is no mention at all of astrology in Peter Singer's thorough study of Galen's ways of explaining things.[6] Be that as it may, we are not concerned here with Galen's overall posture toward astrology, but rather with his role in the development of the medieval astrological understanding of the theory of critical days. We shall not examine his *On Critical Days* directly. Instead, we shall call attention to a critical appraisal of Galen's position found in a new source, never before noticed in the scholarly literature. It is found in the Hebrew version of an epitome of *On Critical Days*, one of the sixteen or so epitomes of Galenic texts that form the so-called *Summa Alexandrinorum*. The Hebrew *Summa* is stated to be a translation from the Arabic.[7] However, the Hebrew version of this particular epitome is entirely different from the Arabic text preserved in MS Princeton, Garrett 1075, the only manuscript to which we have access at present.[8] The Hebrew differs from the Arabic, its purported source, throughout.

We shall look briefly here at the beginning of the third and final book of *On Critical Days*, which, as we have seen, is the chief locus for a discussion of astral connections to human illness. In fact, this Hebrew epitome and pseudo-Ptolemy's *Centiloquium*, read together with Ibn Dayā's commentary (to be discussed in detail below), seem to be, at this juncture at any rate, the two most pivotal texts for the development of the medieval tradition of astrological medicine. Galen's text begins as follows: "Whoever thinks that it is better to consider the reasons why illnesses are not judged on each day, should consider that the following treatise has been composed especially for him. It is appropriate to acknowledge principles for discovering the critical days, just as also has been said in the commentary above. For there are two kinds: namely, experience (*peira*) [and reasoning]" (ed. Kühn, *Claudii Galeni Opera Omnia*, IX, Leipzig, 1825, p. 900. In Kühn's Greek text "and reasoning" is omitted, presumably because it is based on an unreliable manuscript, but *logos* is mentioned in the subsequent discussion).

The Arabic version in MS Princeton follows this closely. Ignoring the recapitulation found in the first two sentences, it begins straightaway with the third sentence: "The principles (*uṣūl*) by means of which knowledge of the critical days can be extracted are two. One is that which can be verified through empirical observation (*bi-mā yashhad bihi al-tajriba*); reasoning (*qiyās*) attests to the other." In stark contrast, the Hebrew version begins as follows: "Book Three. He said, Pythagoras and his school attributed the causes of critical days to the numbers. But to the stars that revolve in heaven they assign attendant events, resulting from their different configurations . . . Galen does think that numbers are connected to this, but they [numbers] are rather figments of human thought, possessing, in his view, no essential reality; nor are they principles. . . ."[9]

Thus the Hebrew version opens with a presentation of the position of the Pythagoreans, followed by a restatement of Galen's view and, finally, by a critical assessment of Galen by the author(s) of the epitome. The Pythagoreans explain the critical days arithmologically; numbers are the basic principles, and they suffice to explain why crises occur on day seven. However, attendant and variable symptoms accompanying the crises are due to the changing stellar configurations. In addition, the Pythagorean theory of critical days is situated within a comprehensive scheme of three worlds: the fixed world, the limited world, and the world below the moon. But even this idea, which connects terrestrial events to superterrestrial entities, has its basis in number: "This is so, because the number three is primeval (*muqdam*), and [so] the worlds were divided up in this manner."

The terms used to signify the three worlds are well known, and their employment by "Pythagoreans" is not surprising. The Hebrew word here translated as "fixed" is *qayyam*, which should derive from the Arabic *qā'im*. This term may be rendered as well by "real." One may hazard a guess that the Greek was *hupostaton*, for the following reasons. First, *hupostaton* (whence the English "hypostasis," so often used nowadays in a variety of manners) can mean "real"; it is so translated consistently by Sambursky and Pines in their study of theories of time, where it appears as the opposite of *anupostaton* or "unreal," whose sources include authors (such as Iamblichus) who are certainly Pythagoreans.[10] Second, the Hebrew and Arabic words, just like the Greek, all derive from a word whose root meaning is "to stand" and thence have acquired the additional, philosophical meanings of "unchanging" and "real." The "limited," in Hebrew *ha-mugbal*, clearly denotes what in Greek philosophy was known as *peperasmenon*, a fundamental Pythagorean notion.[11] The "world below the moon" is standard in all ancient and medieval cosmologies.

Though each of the terms is readily comprehensible, the context within which they are employed is extremely unusual. Many thinkers, including Pythagoreans, saw reality as tripartite. However, for the

Pythagoreans, real/unreal and limited/unlimited are usually pairs of opposites covering all of existence; our author or, to be more precise, his source(s), uses them to name the first two of the three levels of existence. Nonetheless, it certainly makes sense that the fixed, unchanging level should come first, and that the sphere below the moon come last. If the sublunar sphere is thought to be disorderly, random, and the like, then it may qualify as "unlimited," just as the realm of the orderly celestial motions above may be designated "limited."

In sum, though the views summarized by our author are not all out of place for Pythagoreans, it is impossible at this stage of our research to identify by name the Pythagoreans whose views he is summarizing. To be sure, Hippocrates refers to the numerical aspect of critical days.[12] At least one critic of Hippocrates, namely Celsus, asserts that "in these matters indeed the Pythagorean numbers, then quite famous, deceived the ancients."[13] However, the Hippocratic treatises do not claim that the numbers are causes; when explaining why critical days exhibit their peculiar periodicity, they appeal to physiology and pathology—most especially, the time required for the coction of humors. This holds true even for the pseudo-Hippocratic *On Hebdomads*.[14] Aristeides Quintilianus draws a connection between the periods of fevers and palpitations on the-one hand and musical ratios on the other.[15] By contrast, the Pythagoreans of the Hebrew epitome expound their arithmology within the wider context of three worlds or levels of reality; they make no mention of physiology or music.[16]

Furthermore, Hippocrates does not speak at all of the moon or planets in conjunction with critical days. To be sure, the famous statement in *Airs, Waters, Places*, ". . . the contribution of astronomy to medicine is not a very small one but a very great one indeed," was widely cited. As we shall see later on, several Hebrew writers saw in this remark an invitation and a justification for the application of astrology to medicine. Taken in context, however, Hippocrates there refers to nothing more than the seasonal changes that affect human bodily constitutions and, therefore, must be taken into account by medical science. Indeed, the very next sentence reads, "For with the seasons men's diseases, like their digestive organs, suffer change."[17] However, the Pythagoreans of the Hebrew epitome do incorporate astrological considerations into their fundamentally arithmetical theory. Note that the *Theology of Arithmetic*, attributed to Iamblichus, concludes its lengthy discussion of critical days, appropriately placed in the chapter on the number seven, with a jab at the astrologers![18]

In sum, then, at this point we cannot identify the Pythagoreans with whom the author(s) of the Hebrew epitome contrast Galen's ideas. Of course, it may well be the case that the epitome presents its own synthesis of Pythagorean arithmology, astrology, and philosophy.

Galen does not deny the connection between numbers and critical days, but it is certainly not "real" in the way the Pythagoreans maintain.[19] Galen connects critical days to the moon. Specifically, the moon's position with regard to the sun produces general effects, and its position in its own sidereal circuit is responsible for more special effects. The Pythagorean, and especially the Galenic, positions are spelled out in more detail than we can relate here. It seems important to point out, though, that the Hebrew epitome has Galen making a much stronger claim for the stars as causes than would seem warranted from Galen's own writings. Hard-nosed empiricist that he was, Galen recognized a connection between the moon's orbits and critical days (much as he acknowledged the numerical link), but it is by no means sure that he would have seen the stars as a cause, especially when wearing his philosopher's hat.[20]

We should also take into account that not all of the Galenic sources are at our disposal. For example, in his account of his own books, Galen confesses that he wrote "specifically on Hippocrates' views on critical days" in a comprehensive work on "the whole method of healing" that began as an exercise for himself, but which eventually reached a wider audience.[21] Although that work is arranged in fourteen books, it is not identical with his famous *Methodos therapeutike*, which is also in fourteen books.[22] Galen's commentaries on Hippocratic and pseudo-Hippocratic writings should be scoured, especially the Arabic versions, which may display variant texts, reflecting, perhaps, the intervention of medical writers from the critical suture between classical and Islamic civilizations.[23]

After summarizing Galen, the author presents his own evaluation. He rejects Galen's assertion that the moon has no effect during the three days when it is not seen. On the other hand, he praises Galen's explanation of the respective roles of the moon's revolution in its own orbit, and its motion relative to the sun. There is in fact considerably more detail contained in this text, but it can be recovered only after a much closer investigation. The Hebrew translator, Shimsom ben Shlomo, is not known to have translated anything else; his syntax and sentence structure make often for difficult reading.[24] Nonetheless, our reading so far of this striking text certainly indicates that, sometime toward the end of the period conventionally known as late antiquity, there arose a critical assessment of the theory of critical days and its connection to numbers and planets, which, as far as we can tell at the present state of our investigation, attached greater importance to the astral factors than did Galen himself. As we shall soon see, to this development within the "Galenic" tradition there corresponds an elaboration of the "Ptolemaic" tradition in astrology that draws astrology and medicine closer than before.

Applications of astrology to medicine figure in the defense of astrology that Ptolemy presents at the beginning of his *Tetrabiblos*. According to him, it is the Egyptians, "those who have most advanced this faculty of the art," who "have entirely united medicine with astrological prediction."[25] Interestingly enough, Galen also announces his acceptance of the findings of "Egyptian astrologers" in his *On Critical Days*.[26] The Egyptians have devised iatromathematical "systems" (*syntaxeis*) in order "to succeed in learning the qualities of the underlying temperaments, the events that will occur in the future because of the ambient, and their special causes . . .; and, on the other hand, by means of medicine, through their knowledge of what is properly sympathetic or antipathetic in each case, they proceed, as far as possible, to take precautionary measures against impending illness and to prescribe infallible treatment for existing disease."[27]

However, the iatromathematics that is developed later on in the *Tetrabiblos* is quite different from, though not unrelated to, the lunar medical astrology that lies at the heart of *Kelal Qaṭan* and the other Hebrew sources. *Tetrabiblos* III, 12, whose topic is "bodily injuries and diseases," is concerned mainly with general astral indicators, for example, that "in general, Saturn causes his subjects to have cold bellies, increases the phlegm, makes them rheumatic," and so forth.[28] However, we find there neither the detailed and supposedly precise computation of charts that one finds later on in 'Aynzarbī nor the instructions for bloodletting and other purgations in keeping with the phases of the moon that are set out in *Kelal Qaṭan*. Indeed, much of what Ptolemy describes concerns possible injury from external causes (such as arrows) rather than the pathological developments that are the domain of medical theory.

In sum, then, while the *Tetrabiblos* presents the general theoretical underpinnings for astrological medicine, it does not take up the more specific medical issues that are the main concern of David Ben Yom Tov and other medievals. In keeping with the focus of this survey, it may not be amiss to add here a few comments concerning the presence of the *Tetrabiblos* in the Hebrew tradition. To be sure, Hebrew astrology owes a great debt to Ptolemy (and no less to pseudo-Ptolemy; see below). Nonetheless, the *Tetrabiblos* seems to have been little read. In fact, no Hebrew translation exists. All that we have is a brief exposé by Judah ben Solomon, in his encyclopedic *Midrash Ḥokhmah*, to which he adds some remarks of his own. Astrological medicine is left out of his account entirely.[29]

On the other hand, we should call attention to an interesting manuscript of the Arabic version, along with the commentary of 'Alī b. Riḍwān: Escorial 913. The manuscript is written partially in Arabic characters and partially in Hebrew characters. There are marginalia throughout in Judaeo-Arabic, in at least two different hands, mostly in the form of cross-references. This manuscript certainly warrants further study, especially as the glosses promise to reveal much about the wider contexts within which astrology was studied.

Let us then resume our sketch. In fact, it is at very nearly the same time as the anonymous treatise cited above that we find a clear statement concerning the role of the moon's phases. Hephaestio of Thebes, writing in 381, observes as follows:

> One must know that people who have been affected by a disease while the moon moves towards benefics, regain their health if the disease reaches its crisis within the first quartile (i.e., within seven days [from the new moon]), especially if the moon in that quartile in a good condition enters into conjunction with benefics. But if the moon moves toward malefics, she will provoke an intensification [of the disease] until she reaches the point diametrically opposite her initial position. If, together with a malefic, there is also a benefic, remission and intensification will be mixed together. Diseases which occur from the time of the full moon onwards, are milder compared with those occurring from the new moon onwards, because the waning moon sedates the vehemence of the sufferings.[30]

A much fuller statement is found in the commentary of Abū Ja'far Aḥmad ibn Yūsuf ibn Dāya (d. ca. 941) on pseudo-Ptolemy, *Centiloquium*, aphorism 60. This is a particularly important text, in that the author makes a clear statement concerning the historical connection between medical practitioners and astrologers, showing the clear dependence of the former upon the latter for the causal explanation of phenomena that they had ascertained already by means of observation.[31] This key text, which survives in several languages, has yet to be edited or studied in depth. Moritz Steinschneider (who, by the way, justly takes credit for having determined the true author of the commentary; in the Latin versions the commentary is usually attributed merely to "Haly," whom modern scholars had assumed to be 'Alī ibn. Riḍwān, the commentator of the *Tetra-biblos*) presents an enormous amount of information concerning the two Hebrew translations (one from the Arabic, the other from the Latin) and some later elaborations in the Hebrew tradition.[32] As is so often the case, scholarship on the text has not progressed much since Steinschneider's monumental contribution. In keeping with the focus of this essay, I cite from the Hebrew translation (from the Arabic) by Qalonymos ben Qalonymos.[33] First, let us look at the aphorism attributed to Ptolemy.

> Aphorism sixty. Ptolemy said: true crises of diseases—they are the time[s] when the condition of the patient appears to shift quickly, either for better or worse—occur when the moon is at one of the angles [of a square] that is circumscribed by the *sphaera recta*. The change that comes beforehand, and which foretells it, occurs when the moon is at the angles of the octagon (*meshumman*); and that which comes before that occurs when the moon is at the angles] of the sixteen-sided figure. [Moreover, the condition of the patient should be developing normally, with nothing external disturbing him.] (The bracketed passages are not found in the Greek version, but occur in all the medieval Latin versions.)
>
> When you find at one of these angles a beneficent fixed star or planet (Greek: When you find one of these angles made fortunate), it indicates a change for the better. But if you find there a malefic, it indicates a change for the worse (Greek: But when you find it harmed, the opposite [is the case]. The Greek omits the rest of this paragraph), unless the malefic opposes the illness and is within its limit.[34] In these centers (!) the moon indicates ardent illnesses, and the sun chronic illnesses. Likewise for every star, according to its characteristics.[35]

Roughly speaking—clearly the complete text-cum-commentary must be studied closely, in the Arabic versions especially—the astrological theory is founded upon four equally spaced points in the moon's orbit. These represent the crises. The inscribed square is bisected twice, yielding other crucial points which precede the crises, and which indicate its outcome. The astral factors are valid indicators only when the illness runs its usual course, and no external factors affect the condition of the patient. Now let us cite from Abū Ja'far's commentary:

> Comment. In this statement Ptolemy has instructed us concerning the critical days; what it is; how the condition of the patient shall be affected for better or for worse; what will come after it, and its changes, according to order.
>
> The physicians stand more in need of this than do the astrologers. This is because many physicians concur that the-crisis is, as he said, without any resistance on the part of the nature of the disease or the ardent illness, on the fourth, the seventh, the fourteenth, and, in addition, on the twenty-first [days of the illness]. They accepted this by tradition, and without knowledge; they made no claim for its [truth] other than what had transpired in their past experiences.
>
> Ptolemy, however, reveals here its cause and the underlying reason. Illness overwhelms at first, and Nature [i.e., the natural governance of the body] is prevented from having its functions carried out normally. But she will not move herself to defeat illness precisely at the time that it overwhelms her. Instead she will wait until the moon arrives at a position that opposes that [initial] position. The superfluity that is moving within it will not have the strength that it had at the onset of illness. Then she shall rise up and defeat her foe.
>
> It is just as the wise opponent would do against a fool. He will restrain himself when he is weak and in the place where he has no succor, then defeat him in the fourth sign from the one in which the illness commenced.

"Ptolemy" discovered that Nature, in her wise governance of the human body, knows better than to try to resist the illness when it first sets in. Obviously, at that time astral factors are working in the illness's favor. Instead, Nature cunningly waits for the moon to move into quadrature to its position at the onset of illness. It then works against the illness; it is precisely at that time that Nature arouses herself to fight off the disease. The crisis, in short, is a well-timed natural response, which would be less effective earlier or later. The physicians had known all along that the body waits seven days before shaking off the illness, or at least before trying to do so; now they know why.

Richard Lemay has suggested that Abū Ja'far is the author not only of the commentary, but also of the *Centiloquium* itself. If this proves to be true, then Abū Ja'far is in effect crediting himself with the major theoretical (and epistemological) leap described above.[36] In any event, it appears that the links between astrology and medicine in general, and those between the theory of critical days and the moon's phases in particular, were high on the agenda of scientists working in medieval Islamic cultures.[37]

Pseudo-Ptolemy is an important source for David Ben Yom Tov's *Kelal Qaṭan*. Aphorisms 19, 20, 21, and 57 are incorporated into the treatise: the first two are utilized in passage 45, the third in passage 35, and the fourth in passage 52. Abū Ja'far's explanation of the link between astrology and medicine, which we discussed at length above, is reproduced in *Kelal Qaṭan*, passages 56–57. The crucial importance of the planets that aspect the moon, noted in *Centiloquium*, aphorism 60, is recorded as well in *Kelal Qaṭan*, passages 72 and 115. However, pseudo-Ptolemy's instructions to divide the orb into eight and sixteen sections, in order to determine the points that will be indicative of the coming crisis, are not followed by David Ben Yom Tov, nor by any other writer covered in our survey. Instead David adheres to other sources, for example, Abraham Ibn Ezra's *Reshit Ḥokhmah*.[38]

Medical astrology in the Hebrew tradition attained its highest and most influential expression in *Sefer ha-Me'orot* (*Book of the Luminaries*), penned by the twelfth-century polymath Abraham Ibn Ezra, certainly one of the most important astrological writers of all times. Moreover, *Sefer ha-Me'orot* is undoubtedly the single most important source for David Ben Yom Tov. We shall, accordingly, conclude this preliminary conspectus with some remarks on Ibn Ezra's short but very interesting tract.[39] Our attention focuses here on roughly the first third of *Sefer ha-Me'orot*. The remaining two thirds, which comprise the indications of the moon's position, aspects of the planets, and so forth, match *Kelal Qaṭan* by and large, and we shall refer as necessary to correspondences or divergences from Ibn Ezra in our notes to the English translation.

Sefer ha-Me'orot is based on the generally accepted principles establishing lunar influence: the moon's proximity to the Earth, which allows it to exercise greater power over terrestrial events; its association with water and fluids; and its phases. These ideas are formulated as general rules later on in the book, for example (p. 13): "If the disease is caused by an excess in the body, and the moon waxes, this will be difficult. But if it wanes, it will be better. But if the disease is caused by a deficit and the moon wanes, it will be difficult, but if it waxes, it will be better."

However, these same notions are situated within a much broader theory of the action of light, one with close theological connections. In the opening sentences (p. 7) Ibn Ezra speaks of "the great light that God emanated from Himself. He gave it to the great luminary [the sun] to rule over the day; and from the great luminary He caused the light to emanate, giving it to the small luminary [the moon] so that it may rule by night. So also the heavens and all the luminous stars rule together with the small luminary." If I understand correctly, Ibn Ezra here accepts the theory, known from other Hebrew texts, that the sun serves as a node for divine light, which is then relayed throughout the cosmos. In keeping with this idea, the stars are all thought to reflect the sun's light, rather than being self-luminous.[40]

On the other hand, he stridently rejects "the nonsensical doctrine" (*divrei ha-mahbilim*) that critical days have some numerological basis (p. 8), specifically in the unlucky nature of even numbers. It would seem that Ibn Ezra is responding here to the Talmudic fear of even numbers, which has been traced to Babylonian extispicy.[41] As we have seen, the Hippocratic corpus endorses the arithmological approach; however, if anything, odd days were more to be feared in that system.[42] Among early Muslim scientists, al-Kindī accepted arithmological explanations, but the ominous number he gives is also odd: 63, which is the sum of nine cycles of seven days.[43]

Next Ibn Ezra takes up the very irregular nature of the moon's motion; it is therefore only a gross approximation that the moon will be at quadrature to its position at the onset of illness after seven days. Similarly, fourteen days is not a precise measure of the moon's opposing its initial position; nor is 27 or 28 days the exact amount of time required to complete the cycle. We may interject here that the Hippocratic writers, for their part, were well aware of the imprecise nature of the numerical sequences they gave for the crises. Indeed, the *Prognosis* compares the periods of fevers, which cannot be measured exactly in integral numbers of days, with the solar year and lunar month, neither of which is described by an integral number of days.[44]

Ibn Ezra promises to provide a method for determining whether the limit will occur on one of the above-mentioned days or not.[45] Although, as far as I can tell, he does not do just that, he does occasionally instruct us on how to determine whether there will be a true limit, or whether something completely unexpected will occur. Thus in a passage at the end of the book (pp. 18–19) he tells us to calculate the moon's position 90 or 180 equatorial degrees from its position at the beginning of the illness. If then the moon is again aspected by or conjoined with one of the planets that aspected or conjoined with it in its initial position, the limit will be "true," for better or for worse; nothing new will befall the patient. However, if the same planet neither aspects nor conjoins with the moon and (perhaps Ibn Ezra means to say "or"?) a different planet does aspect or conjoin with the moon, something totally unexpected will occur. Whether this will be good or bad for the patient depends on her bodily constitution.

Let us return to the beginning of *Sefer ha-Me'orot*. It may well be that Ibn Ezra added the paragraph on the moon's anomalies to prepare the reader for the inevitable, and somewhat standard, objections to astrological theory. He now sets about to respond to these.

First, neither tertian nor quartan fevers have limits. Presumably, the objector wants to know why this is so. If the moon causes crises, then why not for these fevers as well? The answer is that the moon does not remove the disease; it can only intensify or weaken it.

Next, a very common critique, here formulated in a medical context: How can it be that two people fall ill at the same time, but their crises are different? The reply is no less patent: it all depends upon the constitution of the patient. However, in the medical context, more precise answers are available. For example, the moon may have been joined with Mars at the onset of illness; and one patient may have suffered from a hot fever, while the other was afflicted with a cold fever. Mars, a hot planet, will exacerbate the condition of the former but not affect the latter. (Recall that pseudo-Ptolemy had stated that a malefic will not harm the patient if its properties oppose those of the illness.) In general no two human temperaments are exactly the same, nor are the causes of any one illness exactly the same as those of any other. On top of this, the astrological variables are boundless.

These observations, however, lead one to question the use of astrology at all in medicine. Why make use of a science that is so imprecise and so unreliable? Here too Ibn Ezra relies upon some stock answers. The stars exert some general effects, and these will always be a factor, regardless of the individual variables. Similarly, it is a general rule that the moon's position at the onset of an illness is very significant. To be sure, it would be better if possible to have a complete chart for the moment when disease sets in. But physicians too must rely upon general rules. Strictly speaking, the physician ought to know the patient's pulse, urine chemistry, and other data when he is healthy, so as to be better able to assess the illness. The implication, of course, is that the physician does not. In sum, then, Ibn Ezra establishes that astrology, imprecise as it may be, is of use to the physician, who, in any event, will be applying to a particular patient strictly medical rules that likewise are true only *grosso modo*.

Sefer ha-Me'orot is the most important source for David Ben Yom Tov. Passages 53–54, 67, 82–87, and 89–90 derive directly from Ibn Ezra's tract; often they are literal quotations. In passage 46 Ibn Ezra is mentioned by name; and in passage 27, David follows Ibn Ezra against Ptolemy on a technical matter unrelated to medicine. In terms of the number of early printed editions, Ibn Ezra's *Sefer ha-Me'orot* also proved to be the most popular of his works in the Latin West. It was translated in 1292 by Henry Bate of Malines and printed under the title *De luminaribus seu De diebus creticis* by Erhard Ratdolt in Venice in 1482. An abbreviated version of this text (*Abbreviatio Abrahe avenezre de luminaribus et diebus creticis*) was included within Johannes Ganivetus's *Amicus medicorum*, which was printed in Lyons in 1496, 1508, and 1550; in Rome in 1544 (revised by Michael Angelo Biondo); and in Frankfurt am Main in 1614.[46] A second translation was made by Pietro d'Abano toward the end of the thirteenth century and printed under the title *Liber luminarium et est de cognitione diei cretici seu de cognitione cause crisis* by Peter Liechtenstein in Venice in 1507 in *Abrahe Avenaris Judei . . . in re judiciali opera. . . .* Both translations are presumed to have been made from a French version of the Hebrew text, by Hagin le Juif, which is no longer extant. With this background, we are now ready to turn to the treatise that is the focus of our study, David Ben Yom Tov's *Kelal Qaṭan*.

David Ben Yom Tov, author of *Kelal Qaṭan*

David Ben Yom Tov was a Hebrew scholar who lived in the first half of the fourteenth century. He should not be confused with the Portuguese Jew who had the same proper name and patronymic, David ben Yom Tov ibn Bilia.[47] None of the manuscripts of *Kelal Qaṭan* displays the name "Ibn Bilia," nor is there any indication at all that the author lived in Portugal.[48] On the other hand, there is weighty though circumstantial evidence, to be adduced in the course of our introduction, that argues for the author's having resided in Provence or Catalonia. Our author is related, as either the son or father, to the astronomer Jacob Ben David Po'el Ben Yom Tov Po'el (Bonjorn, Bondoron, also Sen Boniat),[49] a well-known Catalan astronomer who in the year 1361 composed astronomical tables for the latitude of Perpignan.[50] David, the father of the astronomer, appears to have been himself an accomplished astronomer. He was a difficult character, and some records concerning his divorce proceedings have survived. David Bonet Bonjorn, Jacob's son, earned a medical degree at Perpignan. Forcibly converted during the anti-Jewish riots of 1391, he considered emigrating in order to revert to Judaism but later abandoned that plan. In response to David's decision to remain Christian, Profiat Duran wrote his famous satire, *Al tehi ka-Avotekha* (Do Not Be Like Your Fathers).[51]

Manuscripts of *Kelal Qaṭan*

This treatise exists in four manuscripts:

1. Oxford, Bodleian Library, Michael Add. 19 [=Catalogue Neubauer 2042], ff. 9b–11b (א). This manuscript is written in Sephardic cursive script and hails from Provence, late fifteenth century. The text is partly hard to read because of blots of ink. The same manuscript contains on ff. 5–9 another composition on medicine and astronomy, that is, a Hebrew translation of pseudo-Galen's *Prognostica de decubitu ex mathematica scientia*.[52]

2. St. Petersburg, Institute of Oriental Studies, Russian Academy of Science C 76, ff. 164b–165b (ש), written in a Sephardic hand of the fifteenth or sixteenth century. The text is partly illegible because of severe staining.

3. Paris, Bibliothèque Nationale de France, héb. 1065, ff. 99a–104a (פ). This manuscript dating from the fifteenth century contains a collection of astrological texts. *Kelal Qaṭan* is featured on fols 99a–104a.[53]

4. Verona, *Biblioteca Civica* 204 (82.4), ff. 102a–104b (ו), Byzantine hand of the fifteenth century.

MS א has been selected as the base manuscript for the critical edition since it has preserved the best readings. The text of א has been corrected, where this seems appropriate, on the basis of the other three manuscripts.

The Latin Translation

David's treatise exists in a Latin translation that is found in a single manuscript: Barcelona, Biblioteca de Catalunya 634, fols. 84r–90r.[54] In general the Latin text follows the Hebrew text closely and is a reliable witness to it, but sometimes the text has been corrupted through misinterpretation or faulty reading. At other times the text has additional material that does not appear in the Hebrew text, mostly of an explanatory character, while occasionally one gets the impression that the admittedly verbose Hebrew text has been abbreviated. It is hard to say whether the Latin translation goes back to one of the traditions represented by the extant Hebrew manuscripts or is based on a lost Hebrew MS tradition. Although there is a certain congruity with א, at times the Latin text agrees with the other manuscripts. In a few cases we have used the Latin text to emend a corrupt Hebrew text. All deviations from our Hebrew edition have been listed in the critical apparatus to the Hebrew text. Significant differences between the Latin and Hebrew text have been listed in the footnotes to the English translation as well.

Survey of the contents of *Kelal Qaṭan*

In the opening passages [1–6] David Ben Yom Tov establishes the intrinsic relationship between medicine and astrology. Change or movement in the sublunar world is caused by forces issuing from the celestial spheres. Astrology studies the change in the supernal world and its effects below, whereas medicine studies the movement from health to illness and from illness back to health. Hence there is some overlap between the two fields. However, mastery of both is beyond the capability of just about everyone. Such was the case already in the time of Hippocrates; how much more so in the author's own time, when hearts have shrunk to the size of a "very fine needle." David then alludes to his motivations for writing this treatise [7–10]. Physicians rarely have any knowledge of astrology and, therefore, are forced to consult astrologers (or those pretending to be experts in that field) for guidance. In response to a request from a friend (a common topos in medieval literature, but perhaps this may actually have been the case), David agreed to prepare a concise handbook for the use of physicians.

The physician will still need to avail himself of some basic astronomical and astrological data [11–19]. For fruitful use of this guide the physician should first of all learn to compute the positions of the seven planets from the almanac. For most of the planets this is not very difficult; but the motions of Venus and the Moon are more complex, and the physician may wish to commission an expert to make these calculations for him. Other tables containing information "vital for the intention of this treatise" have been added as an appendix. These tables are missing from all four Hebrew manuscripts. However, five tables are displayed in the Latin version. These addenda tabulate various correspondences between astrological data and the human body. To make use of them, the physician needs to know the planetary positions, as stated above.

Interestingly enough, Hebrew versions of three of these tables are found in a manuscript at Chicago, Newberry Library Or. 101: table II (=Or. 101, f. 92a), table IV (=Or. 101, f. 91b), and table V (=Or. 101, ff. 95b–96a). Newberry Library Or. 101 contains a set of the tables of Abraham bar Ḥiyya with many interesting and, occasionally, unique additional materials, including tables drawn up for Narbonne and Montpellier (neither of which is very far from Perpignan). Some of the extra materials in this manuscript are connected to Abraham Ibn Ezra, whose *Sefer ha-Me'orot* is certainly the most important source for *Kelal Qaṭan*.[55]

Then follows a presentation of some basic concepts in astronomy and astrology [20–33]. Finally, in passage 34, David begins to enunciate the rules whose exposition is "the intention of this treatise." The astrological factors all concern choosing the propitious moments ("elections") for therapeutic intervention. Medieval medical theory was very much concerned with eliminating from the body excess fluids, whose retention was thought to be a major cause of disease. In other words, the division of tasks between the two disciplines was simply this: medicine tells us what to do, and astrology tells us when (or when not) to do it. Accordingly, the first and main section of the "concise rule" [34–49] instructs the physician concerning propitious and impropitious times for expurging fluids, either by means of surgery (bloodletting) or drugs (purgatives, emetics, etc.). The position of the Moon is the chief, indeed almost the only, indicator in these questions.

The next section [50–54] outlines astrological indications concerning the physician-patient relationship. Specifically, it spells out possible stellar causes for errors on the physician's part, which recommend that the patient find some other doctor.

Another important component of medieval medicine was the theory of "critical days." David devotes considerable space to this issue [55–75]. Here too the Moon is the chief indicator. This is followed by more general remarks concerning the prognosis. A struggle is portrayed between "nature"—that is, the body's endowed capacity to heal itself—and the disease. Astral factors come into play as influences that either help or hinder medical treatment [76–92]. The treatise ends with a brief apology for the limited precision of the rules given in this treatise. David's treatise does not take into account personal characteristics of the patient, be they astrological (natal horoscope) or religious (deeds of the patient, divine decree). Each of these has some bearing on the patient's ultimate fate.

Astrological Medicine in the Medieval Jewish Tradition

Just how extensive was the interest in astrological medicine on the part of Jewish physicians? To answer this question properly we must first accomplish two things. To begin with, we must take stock of the extant medical-astrological treatises, as well as documents and relevant references in other branches of literature. The second and more difficult task is to agree on a way of assessing the importance of astrology in medical theory and practice; for it must be obvious that simply producing a long list of documents does not prove that it played a significant role. Indeed, at this stage of research, it seems that the following generalization of Haskell Isaacs applies equally well to Hebrew medicine: "On the whole, however, astrology played only a small part in Arabic medicine."[56]

The Cairo Genizah furnishes some very rough statistics. From among more than 1,600 medical and "paramedical" documents listed in a recent catalogue, only about 25 display some clear connection between astrology and medicine.[57] Moreover, none of the detailed horoscopes from the Genizah analyzed in a series of studies by Bernard Goldstein and David Pingree are connected to medical questions.[58] Instead, the medical-astrological documents from the Genizah tend to tabulate general connections, but as a rule do not presuppose or pretend to provide any precise information drawn from either medical or astrological theory.

So much for the Genizah. Not a few codices contain a mixture of amulets, medical recipes, and astrological notices. These belong to "folk medicine" and "folk astrology." However interesting they may be in their own right, they certainly have no bearing on the type of intimate connections between astrology and medicine, particularly in the realm of theory, that we are studying here. A few examples of codices of this type will suffice: Jerusalem, Mossad Ha-Rav Kook 1317; Torino III 12; New York, Columbia University X 893 M 6857; New York, JTSA MS 16030 (in Judaeo-Arabic: Yemen).

Short notes or tables connected to astrology are occasionally inserted into some of the standard medical texts. As a rule, those texts do not take astrological considerations into account. The addenda illustrate the need felt by some physicians to supplement the medical text with some astrology, but they indicate no less the marginal status of astrology in medieval medicine. Here are a few examples; all manuscripts are in Hebrew unless specified otherwise:

(a) Notes on astrology (in Arabic) inserted near the end of a copy (Arabic, transcribed into Hebrew letters) of Ḥunayn ibn Isḥāq's *al-Madkhal fi 'l-Ṭibb* (Vatican, ebr. 348, f. 61a).

(b) Astrological charts added to an index of Ibn Sīnā's *al-Qānūn*, book II (Oxford, Bodleian Library, Opp. 179, f. 121a).

(c) Lists of connections between the zodiacal signs and the human body, added to Bruno de Lungoburgo's treatise on surgery (Vatican ebr. 376, ff. 43a–46a).[59]

(d) Astrological notes added at the beginning and end of a manuscript of Gerard de Solo's commentary to al-Rāzī's *al-Mansūrī* (University of Alabama, Reynolds 5087).[60]

(e) Notes on the connection between zodiacal signs and the body, added to a copy of Natan Falaquera's *Ẓori ha-Guf* (Paris, BNF héb 1192, f. 92b).

(f) A list of days with indications whether or not bloodletting should be performed on them, in Hebrew, inserted in a Judaeo-Arabic copy of Ibn Sīnā's *al-Qānūn*, book two (Munich, arab. 816b, f. 173b).

Lists of days on which bloodletting should be performed or should be avoided form a special subcategory. These recommendations are thought to be based upon the planetary week and its astrological associations. Nonetheless, there is nothing more at play here than simple yes-or-no rules for a given day. One encounters neither the astrological theory (e.g., lunar-planetary conjunctions, terms) nor the medical theory (e.g., critical days) that constitute the core of *Kelal Qaṭan*. Because this scheme of bloodletting days was ostensibly endorsed by Mar Shmuel, one of the great authorities cited in the Talmud, it enjoyed considerable authority among many Jewish physicians.[61]

Another indication concerning the degree of intimacy between astrology and medicine can be found in discussions of the prerequisites for a medical education. David Bonjorn asserts that each of the two professions in truth demands mastery of the other [passages 2–3]. The astrologer ought to know medicine, so that he can apply his theoretical knowledge to some practical end. The medical doctor must know astrology, for both his theoretical (understanding the cause of disease and its progression) and practical (enabling a correct prognosis) accomplishment. However, citing Hippocrates' famous maxim, *ars longa vita brevis*, he observes that no one can really master both disciplines [passage 4].

Not everyone, however, included astrology in the list of sciences necessary for the physician. Maimonides, in his commentary to the first of Hippocrates' famous and widely studied Aphorisms, cites approvingly al-Fārābī's longish disquisition concerning the-sciences that the physician must study; but astrology is not included. Indeed, nowhere at all in his authentic medical writings does Maimonides make use of astrology in the manner of David Bonjorn or any other of the treatises to be discussed presently.

Al-Fārābī, like Maimonides, rejected astrology; and in this direction of thought Maimonides may well have followed the lead of his Muslim predecessor, for whose writings he expresses the greatest esteem.[62] Interestingly enough, though, a manuscript at Paris, BNF héb 1082, f. 33b, preserves, in Judaeo-Arabic, several paragraphs on astrological medicine, said to be copied "from the treatise (*maqāla*) of Abū Nasr al-Fārābī's." Each paragraph describes the "election," that is, the astrologically prescribed time to perform, or not to perform, therapeutic intervention. Purgation, applying an enema, bloodletting, cupping, and cautery each receive one paragraph.

In this connection David Kalonymos's Hebrew translation of John Simon of Zeeland's treatise on the equatorium is not without interest.[63] John Simon states that he designed this instrument especially for the use of medical doctors. As he writes in the opening lines, the equatorium was meant "for the benefit of all those who study the science of astronomy, but especially for the physicians, for whom the science of astronomy is requisite, as Hippocrates said. These are his words in the first book of Prognostic: "Moreover, there is another indication (?) from the orbs, which every doctor should look at closely. . . ." (Paris BNF héb 1051, f. 118b).[64] Furthermore, in a postscript to his translation, Kalonymos mentions having found an equatorium in the possession of a Christian doctor in Trento.

The Hebrew versions of Arnald of Villanova's book on astrological medicine, *De judiciis astronomiae* or *Capitula astrologiae*, make up a very important chapter in our story. Indeed, this is the only Hebrew treatise to go beyond the cycle of the Moon in its astrological analysis. Arnald's book was translated by Shlomo Avigdor in 1393, apparently at Montpellier, under the title *Panim ba-Mishpat*. Steinschneider lists nine copies of this text.[65] A decade earlier Jacob ben Judah Cabret (Qabrit) of Barcelona had prepared an abbreviated recension of Arnald's tract, based upon his own reading of the Latin.[66] Any argument for the importance of astrological medicine in Jewish practice would have to rest strongly on the popularity of Arnald's treatise.

Pertinent as well in this connection are some writings of Bernard de Gordon. The attitude of that important medical writer has recently been studied by Danielle Jacquart.[67] Hebrew translations of Bernard's works were very popular.[68]

Kelal Qaṭan is the most detailed and extensive original Hebrew treatise on astrological medicine. A few other tracts are extant that treat the subject more or less on the same level, that is to say, relying exclusively (or almost so) on the indications of the Moon, though none of them are as extensive or detailed as *Kelal Qaṭan*. One of these is a short tract written by one Pinḥas of Narbonne, concerning whom we have no additional information. Two copies have been identified: Boston, Countway Library of Medicine heb. 2, ff.- 198b–199a, written in a Provençal hand of the fourteenth century; and Oxford, Bodleian Library, Hunt. Donat. 21 [= Neubauer 2130], ff. 296b–297a, dating from around 1470.[69] We present here a synopsis of its contents.

The sublunar world in its entirety is causally contingent upon the stars and planets. However, it is the Moon in particular that holds sway over plants and animals. Hence the author decided to investigate the relationship between the four seven-day cycles of the lunar month and human pathology. He achieved his results empirically (*ba-nissayon*). A key distinction is drawn between "natural" and "accidental" disease. If we understand correctly, a "natural" illness is one in which the increase in bodily fluids (which, according to medieval medical theory, causes diseases) is synchronic with the increase in the size of the lunar disc; if the case is otherwise, then, the disease is labeled "accidental." The author follows the course of the synodic month, offering medical advice, especially with regard to purging (in its various forms).

If the disease occurs on the first day of the phases of the Moon, the disease will be natural. In this case only purgation on the third day—and even better on the fourth day—will be useful, but not on the first two days. The patient should adhere to a healthy regimen in the first three phases of the Moon and beware of everything that is harmful and heavy; there is no need to consult a physician. If the disease occurs in the middle of the first two phases, when the Moon is increasing; that is, from the second day onward, that disease is called accidental. If purgation takes place at the beginning of the disease, the patient will be healed quickly. But if one waits for one or two days, the disease and the nature of the patient will be of the same strength. Therefore, his nature should be strengthened by means of purgation. When the disease occurs in the middle of the last two phases of the Moon, when it is decreasing, and the patient is purged at the beginning of the disease, he will be cured before the arrival of the New Moon. If a disease occurs in the fourth phase of the Moon, purgation should take place on the very same day, for otherwise the patient will be in grave danger. The author concludes by remarking that these general rules only hold good for chronic diseases but not for quartan and tertian fevers.

As for the four quarters of the Moon, if the disease happens in the first quarter it is called natural and if it happens in the middle quarters it is called accidental. If it happens in the beginning of the first quarter or when the Moon is full and purgation takes place on the first or second day, it is dangerous. But if the purgation takes place after the first two days, the patient will be cured. If the disease occurs on the fourth day, the sickening matter will be stronger than nature and overcome it. If there is no purgation through sweat, blood, or vomit on the third, fourth, fifth, or seventh day before the New Moon, there is no hope for the patient. If the disease occurs in the middle of the first or second quarters and purgation takes place on the first or second day, it is a good sign; the patient will be cured without any delay. But if no purgation takes place on these days it is dangerous because nature is then overcome by the accident and the superfluities(?). If the disease happens in the middle of the last two quarters, one should not despair because the patient will be cured in any case with or without purgation before the New Moon.

Let us now briefly survey other manuscript materials related to our subject. An anonymous medical compendium found in a manuscript at Cambridge (CUL Add. 1022.2) discusses connections between medicinal plants and the stars. Two facets of the relationship are spelled out: the days of the lunar month during which a given plant ought to be harvested, and the association between that plant and one of the seven planets. Moreover, the writer raises some of the issues connected with the theory of specific qualities (*segullot*), one of the knottier problems of medieval science. He is interested, of course, in the specific medical properties attributed to certain plants. In his concluding remarks he voices a healthy skepticism (f. 5b):

> Said the author: See now, I have written this, not because I am a believer, but rather in order to know the nature of the secrets of the lofty [bodies?] and the nature of the wonders of the reality that God created—may His name be blessed, He who has potency over everything. I wanted to speak to the accomplished philosophers who are with us today, in order to query them whether there exists a proof for this; or whether it is sensed and accepted (*muḥash u-mefursam*) among them, so that it requires no proof. It would rather have the proof of *segullot*, for which the natural philosopher can find no nature, as Ibn Rushd said.

Our author asserts that the *segulla* is a function of the proportion of the elements making up the plant. The possible proportions are infinite. The infinite is unknowable and, therefore, so also are the causes of the *segullot*.[70]

There are a number of collections of pieces of advice, most of them relating to medical astrology. They do not exhibit the literary structure of a treatise and, in our view, should not be viewed as more than collected notes. Examples are found in Oxford, Bodleian Library, Marsh 410, ff. 81a–84b and Escorial G-IV-9, ff. 144b–145b. Note that both include astrological recommendations that are not connected to medicine: the former has advice on gardening, the latter on clothesmaking.

Finally, we would like to call attention to an extremely interesting Hebrew text by the physician and translator Shem Tov b. Isaac of Tortosa. Shem Tov did not produce a monograph on astrological medicine. However, at several junctures in the introduction to *Sefer ha-Shimmush*, a translation of al-Zahrāwī's *Kitāb al-taṣrīf* which he began to write in 1254, he offers some important observations on the subject. Of special interest are some experiments he conducted in order to isolate and test supposed astral factors.

Two elements play a central role in Shem Tov's analysis. One is the air which we breathe and its corruption through changes in the seasons. Physicians have made use of astrology in order to learn which airs are wholesome and which cause diseases. Hippocrates already stated that diseases have heavenly causes (*yesh ba-ḥoli'im devarim shemeymi'im*) and that therefore a physician should have knowledge of the effects of the planets. This is the reasoning underlying his well-known saying, "that astronomy is not a small part of medicine."[71] Knowledge about the corrupting effect of the planets on the air in the different seasons of the year is—as he remarks—imperative for a physician because then he can purify the body of a patient of the superfluous humor which receives that effect. For example, when the physician knows on the basis of the motion of the planets that they make the air extremely hot, dry, and burning, he should purify the body of a patient of any superfluous yellow bile before it becomes inflamed. Moreover, he should moisten and cool the other humors as much as possible. These preventive measures will safeguard the patient from developing a high fever as a result of the ambient heat and its potential effect on any bilious superfluity in his or her body.[72]

The second central element is the motion of the Moon through the signs of the zodiac. Shem Tov credits Galen with the discovery that the "movements" of diseases always follow the motion of the

Moon.[73] For this reason a physician should know the nature and strength of the signs of the zodiac and the times of the Moon's sojourn in each sign so that he will be careful not to administer a strong purgative when the Moon is in a cold and dry sign or in a hot and dry sign. For when the Moon is in a hot and dry sign, even a small amount of purgative has a strong effect and weakens one's strength. Conversely, when it is in a cold and dry sign it tends to solidify the bodily fluids. Hence even a large amount of a purgative has little or no effect, and, in addition, it will be accompanied by continuous (obstinate, resistant to treatment?-*mamrin*) pains and aches and other symptoms.

It is here that Shem Tov describes his own endeavors to verify this point. He admits that he had thought light of this rule. In order to test it he gave a purgative to a patient when the Moon was in Capricorn (a cold wet sign). Indeed, the patient was afflicted by aches and obstinate (*mamrin*) pains in his stomach, feebleness, and an urge to vomit. However, after the Moon had moved from Capricorn into Aquarius (a warm wet sign), he gave some of the same drug to another patient. It did not have a bad effect on him and none of those afflictions occurred to him. On the basis of this empirical verification, Shem Tov admonishes physicians to take heed of this lesson and always remember that astrology is an important part of the medical art.[74] Moreover, they should make an effort to know the signs the Moon is in for every month and administer a drug at the appropriate time.[75]

Talismanic cures certainly have an astral basis, since the timing of the placement of the talisman and the figures engraved upon it are decided upon by astrological considerations. This type of healing, however, is essentially different from the kind under consideration here. *Kelal Qaṭan*, and the genre to which it appertains, relies solely upon standard (that is, for the most part, Galenic) medical theory for the type of treatment to be employed: phlebotomy, purgation, etc. Astrology enters only as a means of deciding when, or when not, to administer the treatment. By contrast, talismanic medicine employs a totally different mode of treatment—that is, talismans. Nonetheless, we may summarize here the little information we have concerning Jewish interest in this form of therapy.

Thus far only one Hebrew treatise on talismanic medicine has come to our attention: *Megillat ha-Setarim*, preserved uniquely in Paris, BNF héb 1051, ff. 108a–177. This appears to be the work of a Jewish writer, not a translation. It consists of two series of twelve paragraphs, each of which is devoted to one of the zodiacal signs. In the first series, the author states which bodily organ is governed by the sign and describes the figure to be drawn on the talisman. The second series prescribes rules for the application of the talisman, providing the full astrological data necessary for its empowerment.

Likewise, we know of only one report of an actual use of talismans by Jewish physicians. Around the year 1300 Jewish physicians in Montpellier—among them R. Isaac de Lattes—reportedly used astrological talismans for medical purposes. An example of such a talisman is the famous "Lion sigil," made of gold with the engraved image of a woman riding on a lion without a tongue. It was supposed to bring relief to an ailing right kidney. To strengthen its effect, fumigation with mastic was recommended. The practice is reported and severely criticized by Abba Mari in a letter to R. Solomon ben Adret (Rashba) of Barcelona.[76]

Astrological prognostications concerning mass disasters, such as the Black Death, are also only distantly related to our topic. *Kelal Qaṭan* addresses common or uncommon ailments that can affect anyone at any time, and the astrology invoked recommends the timing of therapy applied to individual cases. As such it has little if anything in common with astrological predictions, or post facto explanations, of large-scale events. The physician and philosopher Moses Narboni is one of many scholars, belonging to all three major faiths, who connected the pestilential outbreak with a Jupiter-Saturn conjunction.[77]

Our study leads us to the following conclusions. Astrology played a minor role in Jewish medical practice. Its main application was in choosing proper times for bloodletting or other forms of purgation. Theoretical interest was mostly limited to the connection between the lunar cycle and human pathology. There was a significant burst of interest in the subject in southern France and Catalonia, especially during the fourteenth century; this is true for Latin medicine as well. This activity is reflected in, for instance, the works of Shem Tov Ben Isaac and Pinḥas of Narbonne among Jewish authors and in those of Bartholomew of Bruges, Bernard de Gordon, and Arnau of Villanova among their non-Jewish counterparts. David Ben Yom Tov fits very well into this scheme, geographically and chronologically. The most interesting of the Hebrew treatises, and the only one to attain any significant circulation, judging from the number of extant copies, is the one we publish here, David Ben Yom Tov's *Kelal Qaṭan*.

Postscript: Astral Indications for Ailments of the Eyes

One peculiar element in the chapter from the *Tetrabiblos* discussed above does, however, have a presence in Hebrew letters: Ptolemy's exposition of the astral indicators for ailments of the eyes.

Here, and here alone in this chapter, Ptolemy marks the role played by specific fixed stars; elsewhere, only planets and zodiacal constellations are named. Ptolemy declares, "For blindness in one eye is brought about when the moon by itself is upon the aforesaid angles, or is in conjunction, or is full, and when it is in another aspect that bears a relation to the sun, but applies to one of the star clusters in the zodiac, as for example to the cluster in Cancer, and to the Pleiades of Taurus, to the arrow point of Sagittarius, to the sting of Scorpio, to the parts of Leo around the Coma Berenices, or to the pitcher of Aquarius . . ."[78]

Several manuscript copies of the tables of Abraham Bar Hiyya (eleventh century, Barcelona) contain a set of three short lists of star lists that signify, in one way or another, for the eyes.[79] The first two exhibit information that is not to be found at all in the *Tetrabiblos*. The last bears a double caption. On the right it reads, "The names of the figures that signify for the weakening of eyesight, according to the astrologers (*hakhemei ha-nissayon*) and, according to them, these degrees do not move (*mitgalgalot*)." Fifteen star names are listed underneath, and some of them correspond roughly to the information provided by Ptolemy in the passage cited above. Thus the first star listed is "Pleiades in the sign of Taurus"; the arrow point of Sagittarius, the sting of Scorpio, and the pitcher of Aquarius are also listed. However, as noted, Bar Hiyya lists a total of fifteen stars or asterisms. Moreover, in the column on the left, which is headed, "The measure in degrees of the stars that have the capacity to signify the weakening of eyesight when they are in opposition to the luminaries," supplies the longitudes for the stars listed to the right. No longitudinal values at all are displayed in the *Tetrabiblos*.

Bar Hiyya's table corresponds much more closely with a group of stars, whose longitudes are specified, in an anonymous astrological tract from the year 379. The passage of interest reads: "When the moon is in the node and especially when its light is waning or in the Ascendant at these places and also when the sun is in a similar position near these places, they damage and dim the eyes, even though there is not any testimony of the maleficent stars. These places are, especially, the cluster of Cancer, which is between the eleventh and the fourteenth degree, the Pleiades of Taurus, from the fourth to the sixth degree, the arrow point of Sagittarius, at about the seventh degree of Sagittarius, the nebulosa which is near the eye of Sagittarius that lies in the twenty-eighth degree of this sign, Scorpio's sting which is in the thirtieth degree of this sign, the Coma Berenices of Leo-the southern one at the twenty-seventh degree, and the northern one at the thirtieth degree of Virgo—the pitcher of Aquarius from the seventeenth to the eighteenth degree and the spine of Capricorn from the twenty-fifth to the twenty-eighth degree."[80] Nonetheless, only about half of Bar Hiyya's stars are given here (not to mention the two other tables for which we have identified no other source), and the longitudes occasionally differ as well.

We shall defer any further comparison to a future publication in which Bar Hiyya's tables are presented in full.[81] For now it suffices to observe that Bar Hiyya's tables circulated widely; I have noted fourteen manuscript copies. David Kalonymous, working in Bari, used the Alphonsine Tables in order to update the tables for the year 1496.[82] Other than this, however, there is no sign that these traditions of prognostication for the eyes generated any interest. Unlike the lunar phase-critical day teachings, they can offer no guidance to the physician with regard to courses of action that should be pursued or avoided.

Notes

1. Ptolemy, *Tetrabiblos*, edited and translated by F.E. Robbins (Loeb Classical Library) (Cambridge, USA, and London, 1971), p. 35.

2. Ibid., p. 45.

3. Hippocrates, with an English translation by W.H.S. Jones, 4 vols. (London and New York, 1923–31) vol. 4, p. 115; see n. 2 for criticism of previous translations.

4. This summary is based on the translation of Shem Tov b. Isaac of Tortosa, completed in 1267, and found uniquely in New York, JTSA MS 2720, ff. 13a–b. Hinrich Biesterfeldt and Tzvi Langermann hope to publish soon a preliminary study of Palladius' commentary, to be followed by a full edition and analysis.

5. Tamsyn S. Barton, *Power and Knowledge: Astrology, Physiognomics, and Medicine under the Roman Empire* (Ann Arbor, 1994), p. 54. Barton's criticism is directed specifically at Vivian Nutton in his edition of Galen's *De Praecognitione, Corpus Medicorum Graecorum* 5.8.1. (Berlin, 1979). For a detailed study of the relevant texts, some of which are extant only in Arabic, see Gerald J. Toomer, "Galen on Astrology and Astrologers," *Archive for the History of the Exact Sciences* 32 (1985), 193–206.

6. P.J. Singer, "Levels of Explanation in Galen," *Classical Quarterly* 47 (1997), 525–542.

7. See Moritz Steinschneider, *Die hebraeischen Uebersetzungen des Mittelalters und die Guden als Dolmetscher* (hereafter *HU*) (Berlin, 1893), pp. 654–656.

8. Fuat Sezgin, *Geschichte des arabischen Schrifttums*, III, 149, lists two other manuscripts, both at Teheran.

9. The following manuscripts have been consulted: Parma, Palatina 2919, f.-118b; Vienna cod. heb. 29, f. 203a; Paris BNF héb 884. Manuscripts of the Hebrew translation are discussed by Steinschneider, *HU*, pp. 654–656.

10. S. Sambursky and S. Pines, *The Concept of Time in Late Neoplatonism* (Jerusalem, 1987), glossary (p. 115) and, e.g., citing Iamblichus, top of pp. 28–29.

11. See, e.g., W.K.C. Guthrie, *A History of Greek Philosophy*, vol. 1, *The earlier Presocratics and the Pythagoreans* (Cambridge, 1962), pp. 247–248.

12. See the sources discussed by G.E.R. Lloyd, *The Revolutions of Wisdom: Studies in the Claims and Practice of Ancient Greek Science* (Berkeley, 1987), pp.-264–270. Add to them the extensive discussion in Hippocrates, *On Fleshes*, section 19, in Hippocrates, vol. VIII, edited and translated by Paul Potter (Cambridge and London, 1995), pp. 158–165.

13. Celsus, *De medicina*, with an English translation by W.G. Spencer (Cambridge and London, 1960), I, p. 241.

14. This is stated explicitly in ch. 27 of *On Hebdomads* (W.H. Roscher, *Die hippokratische Schrift von der Siebenzahl in ihrer vierfachen Ueberlieferung*, Paderborn, 1913, pp. 46–48); cf. Lloyd, *Revolutions* (n. 10 above), p. 270 n. 190.

15. Leofranc Holford-Strevens, "The Harmonious Pulse," *Classical Quarterly* 43 (1999) 475–497, at 477–478.

16. 'Alī b. Rabban al-Ṭabarī, *Firdaws al-ḥikma*, ed. M.Z. Siddiqi (Berlin, 1928, pp. 310–311), moves smoothly from the hebdomads, which he cites in the name of Hippocrates, into a theoretical connection between the moon's phases and the progress of diseases (310:12 11.); but no such connection is found in the Hippocratic source, and the conflation is a product of the developments in late antiquity and early Islam, of which we are speaking here.

17. *Hippocrates*, translated by W.H.S. Jones, vol. 1 (Cambridge and London, 1972), p. 73.

18. *The Theology of Arithmetic*, translated by Robin Waterfield (Grand Rapids, 1988), p. 99.

19. The text adds here the following highly intriguing remark: "For this reason he [Galen] lambasted (*na'aṣ*) many tracts of Aristotle's followers who are called Peripatetics."

20. See e.g. Galen, *On Antecedent Causes*, edited with an introduction, translation, and commentary by R.J. Hankinson (Cambridge, 1998); and Singer, "Levels of Explanation in Galen" (n. 6 above). Note that neither study makes any reference at all to astrology and the possible role of the moon as a cause, since this is not an important theme for Galen.

21. From "My own books," in P.J. Singer, *Galen: Selected Works* (Oxford, 1997), p. 15.

22. Singer does not capitalize, italicize, annotate, or indicate in any other way that Galen is referring here to an extant work or one that is known elsewhere by title. No citations from the *Therapeutike* are found in the extensive notes or appendices to Roscher's work on the *Hebdomads*.

23. Note e.g. the Arabic commentary of pseudo-Galen to *On Hebdomads*, preserved in MS Munich, cod. arab. 802, extracts of which are published in Roscher, appendix I.

24. What little information there is on this translator can be found in Steinschneider, *HU*, p. 654.

25. *Tetrabiblos*, I, 3, trans. Robbins, p. 31 (substituting "temperaments" (*synkraseis*) for "temperatures"). "This faculty of the art" refers to prognostication.

26. Barton, *Knowledge and Power* (n. 5 above), p. 54.

27. *Tetrabiblos,* p. 33.

28. Ibid., p. 327.

29. The only discussion of the topic remains that of Steinschneider, *HU,* pp.-525–527. On *Midrash Ḥokhmah* see the articles by Resianne Fontaine, Tony Lévy, and Y. Tzvi Langermann in Steven Harvey (ed.), *The Medieval Hebrew Encyclopedias of Science and Philosophy* (Dordrecht, 2000). For purposes of the present study, Oxford, Bodleian MS Michael 551 has been consulted.

30. Felix Klein-Franke, *Iatromathematics in Islam,* (Hildesheim, 1984), p. 66 (translation slightly altered), citing from Hephaestio Thebanus, *Apotelesmatica,* ed. David Pingree, 2-vols. (Leipzig, 1973–4), I, p. 290.

31. It is interesting to compare Abū Ja'far's claim that physicians, in deciding upon the temporal dimension of fevers, had at their disposal empirical data but no theoretical nexus within to place them, with Mirko D. Grmek's criticism of unnamed historians of medicine in his highly acclaimed book, *Diseases in the Ancient Greek World* (translated from the French by Mireille Muellner and Leonard Muellner, Baltimore and London, 1989), p. 295: "However, the logical process by which the Hippocratic physician constructs his clinical picture only appears to be a matter of pure induction. His glance is not as "virginal" or "objective" as numerous historians of medicine say it is. Actually, his nosography is organized on the basis of the various theoretical presuppositions and risky hypothetical generalizations that also underlie his nosology."

32. The Hebrew translations are discussed by Steinschneider, *HU,* pp. 527–531. Steinschneider established the authorship in a lengthy study, "Yusuf ben Ibrahim und Ahmed ibn Yusuf," *Biblioteca Mathematica,* new series 2 (1888), 49–117. A list of manuscripts of the Arabic original, and some other information as well, can be found in Fuat Sezgin, *Geschichte des arabischen Schrifttums,* vol. VII (Leiden, 1979), p. 157. Tzvi Langermann has also identified a version of the *Centiloquium* with an extensive commentary, Spanish or Portuguese in Hebrew characters, in MS St. Petersburg, Academy C 76, ff. 142a–193a.

33. I have relied primarily on MS Oxford, Oppenheim 763 [=catalogue Neubauer 2009], ff. 63a–65b. I consulted as well MS Vatican ebr. 382, ff. 118a–119a. There are no Hebrew manuscript copies of the *Centiloquium* alone; all contain a version that includes Abū Ja'far's commentary.

34. Hebrew, *bi-gvulo.* However, this seems to be a mistake, as neither the sun nor the moon have "limits" in the signs. The correct term (found in the Latin) is "domain", which in Arabic is *ḥayyiz,* and may possibly have been confused with *ḥadd* ("limit"); orthographically the two words may appear to be similar. A star's being in its domain means that a masculine planet is in a masculine sign, a feminine in a feminine sign.

35. For the moon's "centers", which must mean the same as "angles" in the first paragraph—and "kentron" = "angle" in Greek—in Abū Ma'shar (8 in number), 'Umar ibn al-Farrukhān and Ibn abī-l-Rijāl (12) and al-Kindī (16), see G. Bos and C. Burnett, *Scientific Weather Forecasting in the Middle Ages* (London, 2000), pp.-342–4. "Center" and "angle" are also identified in the Latin translations of *verbum* 60, which agree with the Hebrew, and not with the shorter Greek text.

36. Richard Lemay, "Origin and Success of the *Kitab Thamara* of Abū Ja'far ibn Yūsuf ibn Ibrahīm," *Proceedings of the First International Symposium for the History of Arabic Science* (Aleppo, 1978), 91–107; Sezgin, op. cit., pp. 44–45, asserts

that the *Centiloquium* is certainly not a product of Arabic science, though it is the first known astrological treatise to have been translated into Arabic. Basic textual problems, including the dating of the Greek version, remain unresolved; see most recently, Michele Rinaldi, "Pontano, Trapezunzio ed il Graecus Interpres del Centiloquio pseudo-tolemico," *Atti della Accademia Pontaniana*, N.S. 48, anno accademico 1999 (Napoli, 2000), 127–171.

37. The richest discussion of this topic is to be found in Klein-Franke, *Iatromathematics* (n. 30 above), which publishes, *inter alia*, extracts from Abū Ma'shar's *Great Introduction to Astrology* in Hebrew translation (from MS Paris, BNF heb 1034).

38. See, e.g., passage 33 and our note there.

39. We indicate within parentheses page numbers in the easily available and adequate, though far from faultless, printed version in *Sefer Mishpaṭei ha-Kokhavim*, a collection of Ibn Ezra's astrological treatises issued by Meir Baqal (Jerusalem, 1971). We have consulted a few of the many dozens of manuscript copies of this work.

40. See Y. Tzvi Langermann, "Cosmology and Cosmogony in *Doresh Reshumoth*, a Thirteenth-Century Commentary on the Torah," *Harvard Theological Review* 97 (2004), 199–227.

41. Mark J. Geller, "Akkadian Healing Therapies in the Babylonian Talmud," Max-Planck Institut fur Wissenschaftsgeschichte, preprint 259 (2004), pp.-56–57. However, Hippocrates (*Epidemics*, cited by Grmek, n. 29 above, p. 294) observed in one of his patients that "Exacerbations occurred on even days." In astrology even is always associated with feminine, odd with masculine.

42. See Lloyd, *Revolutions* (n. 10 above), pp. 265–266.

43. Klein-Franke, *Iatromathematics* (n. 28 above), p. 69.

44. Cited by Lloyd, *Revolutions* (n. 12 above), p. 268.

45. Ibn Ezra invariably speaks of the limit (*gevul*) of the illness, rather than its crisis. However, the two terms are interchangeable, at least when speaking of acute diseases, as Galen himself remarks in his *On Regimen in Acute Diseases*; see Galen, *On the Parts of Medicine, On Cohesive Causes, On Regimen in Acute Diseases in accordance with the Theories of Hippocrates*, ed. and trans M. Lyons (Berlin, 1969), p. 82.

46. See Raphael Levy, *The Astrological Works of Abraham ibn Ezra*, Baltimore, 1927, pp. 50–51 (Levy wrongly dates the Ratdolt edition to 1485). For manuscripts of the Latin translations of the *Sefer ha-Me'orot* see L. Thorndike, 'The Latin Translations of the Astrological Tracts of Abraham Avenezra', *Isis*, 35, 1944, pp. 293–302 (at p. 300).

47. On David Ben Yom Tov ibn Bilia cf. *Encyclopaedia Judaica* VIII, col. 1158; Steinschneider, *HU*, par. 502 (p. 806): David ibn Bilia (oder Villa) b. Yomtob. Instead of Ibn Bilia we find Ibn (Ben) Bila (Billa) in: M. Kayserling, *Geschichte der Juden in Portugal* (Leipzig, 1867), p. 68; *Kelalei ha-Higgayon* (MS Bodleian, Mich. 88); Adolph Neubauer, *Catalogue of the Hebrew Manuscripts in the Bodleian Library* (Oxford, 1886, repr. 1994), no. 2168: "R. David Ben R. Yom Tov ha-mekhunneh Ben Bila mi-malkhut Portugal"; Neubauer, ibid.: "David ibn Bila's treatise on logic": Steinschneider, *Catalogus Librorum Hebraeorum in Bibliotheca Bodleiana* (Berlin, 1852–1860, repr. Hildesheim 1964), p.-858: "Billa seu Villa proposui" (referring to *Jüdische Literatur des Mittelalters*, pp.-398, 434). According to H. Gross (*Gallia*

Judaica. Dictionnaire géographique de la France d'après les sources Rabbiniques (Paris, 1897), p. 471) the attribution of *Kelal Qaṭan* to David Ben Yom Tov (Poel) is an error since the true author is David ben Yomtob ibn Billa.

48. *Kelal Qaṭan* calls the author: David Ben Yom Tov (MS א) David Ben Rabbi Yom Tov Po'el (MSS פש) and David Ben Rabbi Yom Tov Po'el *ha-ḥumi* (ו).

49. Acc. to Gross, *Gallia Judaica*, p. 471: "Le nom correct et complet est: "Jacob ben David ben Yomtob Poël, appelé Sen Bonet Bongoron ou Bonjorn."

50. See now the book-length study of José Chabás, *L'Astronomia de Jacob ben David Bonjorn* (Barcelona, 1992), especially chapter two, on the three generations of the Bonjorn family. Steinschneider, *Catalogus Librorum Hebraeorum in Bibliotheca Bodleiana*, p. 858: "Forsan Nostri filius est astronomus Jakob b. David Bong'oron b. Jomtob Poel?"; cf. *HU*, par. 387, pp. 614–616.

51. However, Eduard Feliu has cast doubt in a personal communication with Maud Kozodoy on the identification of the addressee of the satire with David Bonet Bonjorn and suggests that the satire was not intended for him. We thank Maud Kozodoy for her extensive correspondence in this matter.

52. Neubauer, *Catalogue*, and *Supplement of Addenda and Corrigenda* compiled under the direction of Malachi Beit-Arié and edited by R.A. May (Oxford, 1994); Steinschneider, *HU*, par. 423, pp. 665–666.

53. Zotenberg, H. (ed.), *Catalogues des Manuscrits Hébreux et Samaritains de la Bibliothéque Impériale* (Paris, 1866).

54. See Burnett's edition in this volume.

55. For a detailed discussion of this manuscript, see Y. Tzvi Langermann, "Hebrew Astronomy: Deep Soundings from a Rich Tradition," in Helaine Selin (ed.) *Astronomy Across Cultures* (Dordrecht, 2000), 555–584, esp. p. 576.

56. Haskell D. Isaacs, "Arabic medical literature," in M.J.L. Young, J.D. Latham, and R.B. Serjeant, *Religion, Learning, and Science in the 'Abbasid Period* (Cambridge, 1990), p. 363.

57. Haskell D. Isaacs, *Medical and Para-Medical Manuscripts in Cambridge Genizah Collections* (Cambridge, 1994). There are considerably more entries in the indices under "astrology," but upon inspection the great majority of these turn out not to have any connection to medicine.

58. Bernard R. Goldstein and David Pingree, "Horoscopes from the Cairo Genizah," *Journal of Near Eastern Studies* 36(1977), 113–144; "Astrological Almanacs from the Cairo Geniza," *Journal of Near Eastern Studies* 38 (1979), 153–171 and 231–256; "More Horoscopes from the Cairo Genizah," *Proceedings of the American Philosophical Society* 125 (1981), 155–189; "Additional Astrological Almanacs from the Cairo Geniza," *Journal of the American Oriental Society* 103(1983), 673–690.

59. Cf. Steinschneider, *HU*, p. 727.

60. Cf. Steinschneider, *HU*, p. 788.

61. Mar Shmuel's rules are given in Babylonian Talmud, Shabbat 129b.

62. See Y. Tzvi Langermann, "Maimonides' Repudiation of Astrology," *Maimonidean Studies* 2 (1991), 123–158.

63. See Bernard Goldstein, "Descriptions of Astronomical Instruments in Hebrew," in David A. King and George Saliba (eds.), *From Deferent to Equant:*

A-Volume of Studies in History of Science in the Ancient and Medieval Near East in Honor of E.S. Kennedy (New York, 1987), pp. 105–141, at p. 121.

64. Burnett's translation of the Greek in *Prognostica* I.1 (7), ed. H. Kuehlwein, *Hippocratis opera*, I, Leipzig, 1884, p. 79 is "There is something divine that a doctor should know."

65. *HU*, pp. 782–3.

66. *HU*, p. 783. Relying only upon a catalogue description, Steinschneider suggested that another short tract, bearing the title *Megillat ha-Setarim* and extant in a single manuscript (Paris, BNF héb 1051, ff. 108–117), is identical with Cabret's epitome. This turns out to be incorrect; *Megillat ha-Setarim* in fact deals with talismanic medicine. A brief synopsis is provided below.

67. Danielle Jacquart, "Bernard de Gordon et l'astrologie," *Centaurus* 45 (2003) [Bernard R. Goldstein Festschrift], 151–158.

68. *HU*, pp. 785–788. Steinschneider's lists have been considerably augmented by the staff of the Institute of Microfilmed Hebrew Manuscripts, Jerusalem.

69. See Neubauer, *Catalogue*, no. 2130. The texts starts with: "Kelal ma'amar she-ḥibber R. Pinḥas z"l mi-Narbona" (Summary of the treatise which was composed by R. Pinḥas of Narbonne of blessed memory). It is thus not fragmentary as stated by Neubauer and Gross (*Gallia Judaica*, p. 430).

70. On *segullot* see Y. Tzvi Langermann, "Gersonides on the Magnet and the Heat of the Sun," in Gad Freudenthal (ed.), *Studies on Gersonides* (Leiden, 1992), 267–284 [reprinted in idem, *The Jews and the Sciences in the Middle Ages*, Aldershot, 199], esp. pp. 273–274 and note 7, which cites another analogy between the mathematically unknowable and *segullot*. For Ibn Rushd's views see the chapter, "fī al-khāṣṣiyya," in his *al-Kulliyyāt* (Algiers, 1989), pp. 233–241; that chapter deserves a study of its own.

71. Cf. Hippocrates, *Airs, Waters, Places* II (trans. Jones, p. 73): "the contribution of astronomy to medicine is not a very small one"; Abū Ma'shar quotes the same sentence from Hippocrates in *Great Introduction* bk I, ch. 5 [38], and continues in this chapter and the next to show the importance of a knowledge of astrology for the physician. The relevant sections are translated as an appendix in F. Klein-Franke, *Iatromathematics in Islam* (no. 30 above), p. 131.

72. MS Paris BNF 1162 (p. 7, col. b; own pagination).

73. MS Paris BNF 1162 (p. 3, col. a).

74. Compare the experiment performed by Bernard de Gordon, described by Jacquart, p. 152. Note also Gersonides' procedure aimed at isolating and thereby identifying an astrological factor, described by Tzvi Langermann in his essay, "Gersonides on Astrology," appended to Levi ben Gershom, *The Wars of the Lord*, translated by Seymour Feldman, vol. 3 (Philadelphia and New York, 1999), p.-510.

75. MS Paris BNF 1162 (p. 5, col. a); cf. p. 8 (col. a) where he remarks that a physician should have knowledge of the mansions of the Moon and the four seasons of the year with their appropriate regimen.

76. Sefer *Minḥat qena'ot*, pp. 20–21, 32. Our report is based upon Joseph Shatzmiller, "In search of the "Book of Figures": Medicine and astrology in Montpellier at the turn of the fourteenth century," *AJS Review*, vol. 7–8 (1982–1983), 383–407.

77. Gerrit Bos, "R. Moshe Narboni, Philosopher and physician," *Medieval Encounters,* vol. 1, no. 2 (1995): 219–251; pp. 240–243.

78. *Tetrabiblos* (Robbins), p. 321.

79. In fact there are four tables; our remarks here are based upon the tables in MS Chicago, Newberry Library, Or. 101, ff. 81b-83a. The third of these, according to the caption, does not signify for the eyes, but rather indicates death or illness. See also the following note. Langermann hopes to publish these tables in a separate study.

80. F. Cumont *et al., Corpus Codicorum Astrologorum Graecorum,* vol. 5.1, pp. 208–209; English translation with helpful notes accessible on-line at <<http://www.cieloterra.it/eng/eng.testi.379/eng.379.html>>, slightly modified here.

81. Still we note in passing that the table displayed in al-Biruni's *al-Tafhīm,* (*The Book of Instruction in the Elements of Astrology,* translated by R. Ramsay Wright, London, 1934, pp. 274–275) resembles that of Bar Hiyya but is not identical with it, nor is it identical to the classical sources discussed above.

82. The manuscript (Parma De Rossi 336) is described very fully in Benjamin Richler, *Hebrew Manuscripts in the Biblioteca Palatina in Parma* (Jerusalem, 2001), pp. 435–436.

Chapter Two

Original Hebrew Text

נאם דוד בן[1] יום טוב[2] [1] לפי שכבר[3] התבאר[4] שהצורות[5] שבעולם[6]
ההרכבה נשמעות[7] לצורות הגלגליות[8] ומהם יקבלו כל רושם ושנוי[9]
בהם איזה[10] מין היה ממיני השנוי. וחכמת הכוכבים ר״ל החלק
העיוני[11] ממנה אמנם תעיין בצדדים אשר בם יפול[12] השנוי בעולם
היסודות מהכח הגלגליי והיתה התנועה מן הבריאות אל החולי ומן
החולי אל הבריאות שני ומלאכת הרפואה[13] אמנם[14] תעיין בשנוי
הזה אשר[15] יכנס[16] בגופות יחויב[17] א״כ שיהיה התיחסות ושתוף
בין אלו[18] שתי המלאכות ר״ל מלאכת הרפואה והחלק מחכמת[19]
הכוכבים אשר קדם זכרו. [2] וכמו שמשלמות[20] ההובר[21] הידיעה[22]
במלאכת הרפואה ובטבעיי[23] האישים והדברים הרפואיים כדי שבהם
יוכל לעזור בכח[24] הגלגלים[25] ולהכין[26] המתפעלים[27]
לקבל פעולת[28] הפועלים או לדחות הרבה[29] מפעולת[30] הפועלים
כשירצה זה[31] [3] כן משלמות[32] הרופא שידע בכחות הגלגליות
ושמושם באישים כדי[33]

---

[1]בן: ב״ר ‪פ‬ ‪ש‬:
[2]טוב: פועל add. ‪פ‬ פועל ז״ל ‪ש‬ add. החומי (!) ‪ו‬ add.
[3]שכבר: ש- ‪ש‬ שכבר התבאר ‪פ‬ ut dicit Tolomeus in Centiloquio L
[4]התבאר: בנסיון ‪פ‬ add.
[5]שהצורות: שצורות ‪א‬ vultus L
[6]שבעולם: אשר בעולם ‪וש‬ שבעולם ההרכבה: huius seculi L
[7]נשמעות: נשמעת ‪פ‬ similes L
[8]הגלגליות: בגלגליות ‪פ‬
[9]ושנוי בהם: שבהם ‪ופ‬ in eis L
[10]איזה: רושם ‪א‬ add.
[11]העיוני: הנסיוני ‪ופש‬ experimentalis L
[12]יפול: תפול ‪פ‬
[13]הרפואה: הרפואיית ‪ו‬ scientie medicine L
[14]אמנם: ‪פ‬ om.

35

שידע להבין¹ הפועלים הרחוקים והקרובים² לפעול במתפעלים
וגם המתפעלים³ יוכנו⁴ אל זה וכדי שבזה יוכל⁵ להקדים הידיעה
בבחרנים הטובים או⁶ הרעים יתר⁷ על ידיעתו מצד⁸ מלכאתו. ובזה
לא יסופק אחד מן החכמים גם לא אחד מאנשי⁹ ההמון. [4] אמנם
לפי¹⁰ שהחיים¹¹ קצרים כמו¹² שאמר¹³ אבוקרט וכל אחד¹⁴ מאלו
המלאכות ארוכה¹⁵ לא תשלם ולא יגיע לתכלית¹⁶ אחת¹⁷ מהם כי¹⁸
אם בחלקים רבים לא יספיקו¹⁹ חיי²⁰ אחד מן האנשים להקיף²¹
אותם החלקים כלם על השלמות כל שכן שאי אפשר שיספיקו²²
חיי אחד מן האנשים להגיע²³ לתכלית²⁴ שתיהן²⁵ [5] עם היות
שנתמעטו²⁶ הלבבות ולבן²⁷ של אחרונים כמחט סדקית²⁸ לזה²⁹ אי
אפשר שימצא אחד מן האנשים מקיף בשתיהן³⁰ ואם ימצא הנה³¹
הוא בפליאה ועל³² זרות.³³

---

¹⁵אשר יכנס: הנכנס פ

¹⁶יכנס: add. L sepe

¹⁷יחויב: חויב ו יתחייב פ

¹⁸אלו: אלה פ אלו שתי: שתי אלה ו

¹⁹מחכמת: מחכמות פ

²⁰שמשלמות: ששלמות פ

²¹ההחובר: הוא פש add.

²²הידיעה: שידע (corrected by a later hand above the line)

²³ובטבעי האישים: והדבדים האישיים ו add.

²⁴בכח: לכח ו virtutes L

²⁵בכח הגלגלים: לכח הגלגלי א כח הגלגל פ

²⁶ולהכין: להכין פ

²⁷המתפעלים: מתפעלים ו המתפעל פ

²⁸פעולת: פעולות פ

²⁹הרבה: הסבה ו

³⁰מפעולות: מפעולות אפ

³¹זה: facere L

³²משלמות: לשלמות פ

³³כדי: בהם ש add.

¹להבין: להכין פ = disponere L

²והקרובים: הקרובים והרחוקים ו הקרובים פ

³המתפעלים: מתפעלים פ

⁴יוכנו אל זה: emendation Bos-Langermann יובנו אל זה ש יורנו על זה פ
הובנו אל זה א dispositi L (= יוכנו)

⁵יוכל: ידע פ (= sciat L)

---

[6]או: ו- פ (- L et)

[7]יתר: יותר פ

[8]מצד מלכאתו ש om. מזה במלאכתו ו מזה מלכתו פ

[9]מאנשי: מבני ש

[10]לפי: דעת ו add.

[11]שהחיים: שחיים ש

[12]כמו שאמר אבוקרט: .L om

[13]שאמר: שיאמר ופ

[14]אחד: אחת ו

[15]ארוכה: add. L multum

[16]לתכלית: תכלית אפ

[17]אחת: אחד ש

[18]כי אם בחלקים רבים: nisi cum multis laboribus et periculis L

[19]יספיקו: יספיק פ

[20]חיי: .L om אא

[21]להקיף: להשיג ו

[22]שיספיקו: שיגיעו פ

[23]להגיע: להשיג ו שיגיע פ

[24]לתכלית: תכלית ו

[25]שתיהן: ambarum scientiarum L

[26]שנתמעטו הלבבות: quia corda hominum sunt debilitata L

[27]ולבן של אחרונים כמחט סדקית: .L om

[28]סדקית: הסדקית ו סדקיות ש

[29]לזה: ולזה ש לזה...זרות: .L om

[30]בשתיהן: לשתיהן א

[31]הנה: .ו om

[32]ועל: ובדרך ו ודרך פ

[33]זרות: זרות א delevit זירוז א (!) correxit

[6] והטוב הוא[1] לכל[2] אדם שיהיה בעל[3] חכמה אחת משידע זעיר
שם זעיר שם ולכן מעט הוא[4] שימצא רופא שידע בחכמת הכוכבים
ואם הוא הכרחי למלאכתו[5] כמו[6] שנאמר[7] [7] ולפעמים ילכו[8] אצל[9]
היודעים בה או[10] שחשבו[11] שהם יודעים בה[12] ועל[13] פיהם ישתמשו
בבחירת העתים לעשות מעשיהם. [8] ולכן[14] אחד מהאוהבים
הנכבדים בקיאים[15] ברפואה אשר בזמנינו[16] זה שאל מעמדי לפי
שחשב[17] כי מה שאינו לחבר לו כלל קטן במה שיצטרך הרופא[18]
יום יום בנתינת המשלשלים והמשקים[19] והמקיאים וההקזות אל[20]
חכמת[21] הכוכבים לפי שאלו[22] העניינים הם תמידיים[23] ויצטרך
עיון גדול בעשיתם[24] כדי שתצליח מלכאתו[25] בם. [9] ואני[26] ידעתי
שבאמרי[27] לא[28] אדע לא[29] אקיים שאדע[30] כי[31] נתפרסם שלא אדע
ועם היותי[32] מכיר ערכי מאנתי(?)[33] להשיב פניו פן יחשבני[34] ממאן
להפיק רצונו [10] ונעתרתי[35] למלאת את[36]

---

[1] הוא: om. ש

[2] לכל אדם: homini L

[3] בעל: ב- ש

[4] הוא: רופא ש add.

[5] למלאכתו: במלאכתו א in medicina L

[6] כמו שנאמר: om. L

[7] שנאמר: שאמרנו ו שיאמי ש

[8] ילכו: medici vadunt L

[9] אצל היודעים בה או שחשב שהם יודעים בה:
ad illos quos credunt scire in scientia stellarum L

[10] או שחשבו שהם יודעים בה: om. פ. או שיחשבו שידעו בה ש

[11] שחשבו: שיחשבו ו

[12] בה: in scientia stellarum L

[13] ועל ש ועל...מעשיהם: et eorum dicto vel consilio se regunt in electione
temporum ad faciendum opera sua L

[14] ולכן: ולזה ופש

[15] בקיאים: הבקיאים וש בקיאים...בזמנינו זה: om. L

[16] בזמנינו זה: בזמננו פ

[17] שחשב כי מה שאינו: aliquid sentire in dicta scientia L

[18] הרופא: בו פ

[19] והמשקים והמקיאים: inv. ו

[20] אל חכמת הכוכבים: quia in talibus indiget scientia stellarum L

[21] חכמת: חכמ'ת פ

[22] שאלו: שבאלו ש

[23] תמידיים: תמידם (?) א תמידים ש

שאלתו כפי¹ מה שהשיגה ידי מהספרים המחוברים בזה² לא
שחדשתי בזה³ דבר מעצמי ומלבי וזה⁴ החלי לעשות⁵ ובאל⁶ אעזר.
[11] ואומר⁷ כל מי שיצטרך⁸ להשתמש בזה⁹ הכלל¹⁰ הקטן יצטרך¹¹
שילמד¹² תחלה לחשוב מקומות שבעת¹³ הכוכבים בכל יום¹⁴ מן¹⁵
האלמנך [12] וידיעת זה קלה מאד אף למי שאין לו¹⁶ מאומה מן
העיון¹⁷ [13] ובפרט מהחמשה¹⁸ הכוכבים שהם¹⁹ שצמחכ²⁰ שידיעת
מקומותם²¹ קלה²² מאד ובדרך קצרה²³. [14] אמנם נגה ולבנה דרך
חשבונם קשה ומבולבל מעט למי שלא הרגיל בזה ולזה²⁴
יצטרך אם²⁵ להרגל מה בידיעת החשבון למי שירצה לדקדק
חשבונם האמתי [15] או שיהיו נחשבים²⁶ אצלו מקומות²⁷ הכוכבים
ההם²⁸ לימים רבים ושנים אשר²⁹ גם זה אפשר³⁰ שיושג בקלות
מהיודעים בזה. [16] גם יצטרך שיהיה אצלו קונדריס הלוחות
הנהוג³¹ לחברו בסוף האלמנך אשר³² הוציאוהו חכמי המשפט דרך³³
קצור³⁴ מספרי³⁵

---

²⁴בעשיתם: במעשיהם ש
²⁵מלכאתו: שם פ add.
²⁶ואני...למלאת את שאלתו: Et propterea volens ei obedire L
²⁷שבאמרו: שאמרי כי באמרי פ
²⁸לא אדע: א om.
²⁹לא: ולא פ
³⁰שאדע: כי אדע ופ
³¹כי נתפרסם שלא: למה שנתפרסם כי לא ופש
³²היותי: היות כי ש
³³מאנתי (?) להשיב פניו: כי לא רציתי להשיב פניו ריקם פ מאתי להשיב פניו ש
³⁴יחשבני: אחשב ופ
³⁵ונעתרתי: ונתערתי פ וחקרתי ש
³⁶את: ופ om.
¹כפי מה ש-: כפי אשר פ כפי מה שהשיגה ידי: iuxta mee scientie paucitatem L
²בזה: א om. לזה וש
³בזה דבר: פ inv.
⁴וזה החלי לעשות: Lפ om. וזה החלי ש
⁵לעשות: ו om.
⁶ובאל אעזר: בעזרת אלהי ש sine quo factum est nichil add. L
⁷ואומר: ו add. כי פ תחלה add.
⁸שיצטרך: שירצה ופ volens L add.
⁹בזה הכלל הקטן: בכלל הקטן פ
¹⁰הכלל הקטן: tractatu L
¹¹יצטרך: מן הצורך אליו ו לדעת פ add.
¹²שילמד: שלמד ו שידע ש

[13] שבעת הכוכבים : השבעה כוכבי לכת **ופ** הז' כוכבים **ש**

[14] יום: שירצה **פ** .add

[15] מן: מ- **ו** האלמנך: האלמנק **ו** passim

[16] לו: **ש** .om

[17] העיון: in scientia astrologie add. **L**

[18] מהחמשה הכוכבים: מהחמשה כוכבים **ו** מחמשה כוכבים **פ**

[19] שהם: והם **ש**

[20] שצמחכ: שצמחן **ש**

[21] מקומותם: חשבון זה מקומותם מן האלמנק **ו** .add מהאלמנך **ש** .add

[22] קלה: עד **א** .add

[23] קצרה: cum almanaco add. **L**

[24] ולזה יצטרך אם להרגל: ויצטרך אם להרגילו **ופ** ולא יצטרך כי (**ש**[1]) אם
להרגל **ש** ולזה יצטרך אם להרגל מה בידיעת החשבון:
Ideo est necesse uti computare illud **L**

[25] אם: **ש**[1]?

[26] נחשבים אצלו: **פ** .inv

[27] מקומות הכוכבים ההם: **ו** .om

[28] ההם: כי הם **א** הם **ש**

[29] אשר גם זה אפשר שיושג בקלות מהיודעים בזה: per illos qui id computare sciunt **L**

[30] אפשר שיושג: יושג **א**

[31] הנהוג לחברו: **ש** .om

[32] אשר: quem sistrenum **L**

[33] דרך בדרך **ו**

[34] קצור: קצר(?) **א**

[35] מספרי החכמה: מחכמת התקנה(?) **א**

החכמה אשר ממנו[1] יודע בקצור וקלות טבעי המזלות והכוכבים
ובתיהם ורומם ושפלותם וכבודם ושנאתם וקלונם ושלישותם
וגבולם ופניהם [17] ויתר הדברים הצריכים לזה המאמר אמנם[2]
לפי שקונדריס[3] הלוחות[4] אינו[5] מצוי אצל[6] כל אדם רציתי לבחור
מהלוחות ההם ההכרחי[7] אל[8] זה המאמר כפי המכוון ממנו[9] בו
[18] ומעט הוא[10] מה שנתערב במה שבחרתי[11] שאינו[12] הכרחי
אל[13] זה המאמר וחברתיו[14] אל זה המאמר כדי שלא יצטרך מי[15]
שיש[16] בידו זה[17] המאמר לחפש אחר הלוחות ההם[18] ולא יצטרך
עם זה המאמר רק לדעת מקומות הכוכבים באחד מהדרכים[19]
הנזכרים[20]. [19] ואחר[21] שיהיה אפשר לו לדעת מקומות הכוכבים
באי[22] מהדרכים הנזכרים ויתר הדברים הצריכים לדעת כפי כונת
זה המאמר יוכל להשתמש על פי עצמו בבחירת העתים הנאותים[23]
להקזות ולמשלשלים ולהקאות[24] מבלי שיצטרך[25] לשאול אל[26] זה
האצטגנין[27] ובעל נסיון בחכמת הכוכבים.

---

[1]ממנו: מהם ו

[2]אמנם: .om פ

[3]שקונדריס: שקנדרס פ שקנדריס ש

[4]הלוחות: הנזכרות ו add. חנזכרים פ .add

[5]אינו: איננו ו

[6]אצל: ביד פ

[7]ההכרחי: הזכירה (=*+הצריכה) ש

[8]אל: ל- פ

[9]ממנו: .om ופש

[10]הוא: .om פ

[11]שבחרתי: שחברתי ו

[12]שאינו: שהוא ש

[13]אל: ל- ו ב- פ

[14]וחברתיו אל: וחברנו ל- ש et adiunxi dictum sistrenum L

[15]מי: מה ש

[16]שיש: שיהיה ופש

[17]זה: .om פ וזה ש

[18]ההם: .om פ

[19]מהדרכים: de duobus modis L

[20]הנזכרים: ההם ו

[21]ואחר...הנזכרים: .om א

[22]באי: בכל יום כפי אחד ו כפי אחד ש באי מהדרכים הנזכרים: .om L

[23]הנאותים להקזות ולמשלשלים ולהקאות: לנתינת המשקים והמשלשלים ועשיית
ההקזות ש הנאתים במשלשלים ולהקזות וליתר הדברים פ
convenientium flebotomiis, purgationibus, laxativis et vomitivis L

[20] ואחר שהוצע מה שצריך[1] שיודע למי שירצה להשתמש בזה
המאמר אתחיל במה שאליו הכונה ואקדים[2] תחלה באור המלות
הנופלות בזה המאמר אשר ישתמשו בהם בעלי זאת החכמה.
[21] יאמר שהכוכב עם כוכב אחר כשיהיה[3] עמו במזל אחד ויהיה
כל אחד מהם בכח גוף האחר וכח גוף כל אחד מהכוכבים ימצא
בלוחות המחוברות[4] עם האלמנך אשר קדם זכרם. [22] מבט[5]
רביעית[6] הוא כשיהיה[7] בין כוכב[8] לכוכב צ׳ מעלות[9] ומבט נכח ק״פ
מעלות[10] ומבט[11] שלישית ק״כ[12] ומבט[13] ששית ס׳[14]. [23] וכל
אלו המבטים יש להם כח המבט[15] אע״פ[16] שיחסרו[17] מהמבט
פחות[18] מי׳ מעלות אם לפניו ואם[19] לאחריו [24] כמו שיהיה בין
כוכב לכוכב צו׳[20] מעלות או פד׳[21] הנה[22] זה מבט רביעית אלא
שאינו הזק[23] כל כוכב כמו[24] שהוא כשהוא מבט שלם וההקש[25] על
זה בשאר המבטים. [25] יאמר בכוכב שהוא נותן הכח כשיהיה[26]
הכוכב[27] ביתו או בבית[28] כבודו או בבית[29] שלישותו או בגבולו
או בפניו ויתחבר עם כוכב אחר או יביט אליו. והבתים והכבוד
והשלישות
והגבול[30] והפנים[31] כל זה יודע מהלוחות המחוברות[32] עם

---

[24] ולהקאות: emendation Bos-Langermann ולהקזות א

[25] שיצטרך: לזה ו add. בזה פש add.

[26] אל: לא(?) א ש om.

[27] האצטגנין: לאצטגנין ש הצטגנין פ א: האצטגנין ובעל נסיון ו האצטגנין או לבעל נסיון: אצטגנין או לבעל נסיון ו האצטגנין ובעל נסיון בחכמת הכוכבים: alicuius L

[1] שצריך: שיצטרך ו

[2] ואקדים תחלה: א[1] ונקדים תחלה ש

[3] כשיהיה עמו במזל אחד: vel unum planetarum cum alio quando est cum ea vel eo in eodem signo L

[4] המחוברות עם האלמנך: om. L

[5] מבט: ומבט פ

[6] רביעית: om. ש

[7] כשיהיה: שיהיה פש

[8] כוכב לכוכב: לכוכב אחד ו כל ככב ש

[9] מעלות: וזה מבט רביעי והוא חצי איבה ש add.

[10] מעלות: והוא מבט איבה גמורה ש add.

[11] ומבט שלישית: המבט השלישית פ

[12] ק״כ: מעלות והוא מבט אהבה גמורה ש add.

[13] ומבט: מבט פ

[14] ס׳: מעלות והוא חצי אהבה ש add.

[15] המבט: מבט פ

[26] הצומח יקרא המזל העולה בפאת המזרח[1] בכל שעה[2] ויודע[3] מתוך הכלים[4] או מתוך הלוחות או יודע בקרוב משעות היום כאשר יתוסף על מעלת השמש לכל שתי שעות[5] שעברו מעת[6] הזריחה מזל[7] אחד אלא שיש בזה קרוב גדול ואי אפשר לכוון אלא מתוך הלוחות או מתוך[8] הכלים.[9] [27] בעל הצומח יקרא מי[10] שהוא בעל[11] המזל הצומח.[12] הכוכב הנקרא[13] שבאחורנית או נזור יודע מהאלמנאך.[14] הכוכב[15] העולה בגלגל גבהותו או יורד בו יודע בדרך זה. מעלת הגבהות תודע[16] מהלוחות הנזכרות[17] המחוברות[18] לאלמנאך.[19] [28] וכשהוא[20] לפני מעלת הגבהות פחות[21] מצי מעלות יקרא עולה וכשהוא אחר מעלת הגבהות פחות[22] מצי מעלות יקרא יורד. מעלת השפלות[23] נכח מעלת הגבהות. [29] הכוכבים הטובים או המצליחים הם צדק ונגה[24] וחמה[25] ולבנה כשלא יהיה ללבנה אחת מן הרעות הכתובות מטה. וכן צדק ונגה וחמה אע״פ[26] שהם טובים ברוב אפשר[27] שיחלש[28] כחם וטובתם.[29] המזיקים הם שבתאי ומאדים וכוכב הוא מזיק על הרוב. [30] יקרא[30] הבית השביעי המזל שהוא[31] נכח המזל[32]

---

[16] אע״פי: אע״פ **פש**

[17] שיחסרו מהמבט פחות: שיחסרום **פ**

[18] פחות מ׳ מעלות: sex gradus vel minus L

[19] ואם: אם **פש**

[20] צו׳: צד׳ **ש**

[21] פד׳: פו׳ **ש** אע״פי שיחסרו ד׳ מעלות אם לפניו אם לאחריו כמו שיהיה בין כוכב לכוכב צ״ד מעלות או פ״ז מעלות **ו** add.

[22] הנה: היה **א**

[23] חזק כל כוכב: כל כך נזק **פ** כל כך חזק **וש** est ita fortis L

[24] כמו שהוא כשהוא מבט שלם: emendation Bos-Langermann כמו שהוא כשהוא מבט שלישית מבט שלם **א** כמו שהוא במבט שלם **פ** כמו שהוא מבט שלם **ש** sicut quando est aspectus completus L

[25] והההקש: והקש **ש**

[26] כשיהיה: כאשר יהיה **פ**

[27] הכוכב: om. **ו**

[28] בבית: om. L

[29] בבית: om. L

[30] והגבול: וגבול **ש**

[31] והפנים: ופנים **פש** כשאר **ו** add.

[32] המחוברות עם האלמנאך: supradictas L

[33] האלמנאך: האלמנך **פש**

[1] המזרח: מזרח **פש**

[2] שעה: שנה **פ**

[3] ויודע: זה **ש** leviter add. L add.

[4] הכלים: בקלות **ופש** add. **א** ditt

⁵שעות: מזל אחד **א** add.

⁶מעת: משעת **פ**

⁷מזל אחד: **ו** om.

⁸מתוך: **ו** om.

⁹הכלים: **פ** om.

¹⁰מי: planeta L

¹¹בעל: בית **ש** add.

¹²הצומח: **פ** om.

¹³הנקרא: quando est L

¹⁴מהאלמנאך: מהאלמנך **פש**

¹⁵הכוכב: כוכב **פ**

¹⁶תודע: **פ** om.

¹⁷הנזכרות: שקדם זכרם **ו**

¹⁸המחוברות לאלמנאך: **L** om.

¹⁹לאלמנאך: לאלמנך **פש**

²⁰וכשהוא: בא **פ** add.

²¹פחות מצי מעלות...פחות מצי מעלות: צי מעלות או פחות **פ**

²²פחות מצי מעלות: צי מעלות ‹או› פחות מצי מעלות **ש**

²³השפלות: descensus sive bisextus L

²⁴ונגה: נוגה ו**פ**

²⁵וחמה: חמה **פש**

²⁶אע״פ: אע״פ **פש**

²⁷אפשר: אי אפשר **א** האיפשי **ש**

²⁸שיחלש: שיחדש **פ** interdum aliquantulum add. L

²⁹וטובתם: וטובותם **פש** om. L

³⁰יקרא: ויקרא **פ**

³¹שהוא: אשר הוא **פ**

³²המזל: **פ** om.

הצומח. יאמר בכוכב[1] שהוא בבית שנאתו כשיהיה במזל נכח
ביתו. [31] יקראו[2] מזלות[3] מתהפכים טלה[4] ומאזנים וסרטן וגדי.
ומזלות עומדים שור[5] ואריה ועקרב ודלי. ומזלות שני גופים תאומים[6]
ובתולה קשת ודגים. [32] יאמר[7] בכוכב שהוא ממתין בהליכתו[8]
כשיהיה מהלך[9] ביום אחד פחות ממהלכו האמצעי שהוא לשבתאי
בי[10] ראשונים אי[11] שני.[12] ומהיר כשיהיה מהלכו[13] ביום אחד יותר
ממהלכו האמצאי. ומהלך[14] האמצעי ללבנה ייג מעלות יי ראשונים.
[33] רעת[15] הלבנה על פנים רבים[16]: אי שתהיה נקדרת. בי שתהיה
קרובה מהשמש פחות מייב מעלות הולכת אליו או מתפרדת ממנו.
גי שיהיה בינה[17] ובין מעלת הנכח פחות מייב מעלות לפניו או
לאחריו. די שתהיה[18] עם המזיקים במחברת או במבט. הי שתהיה
עם כח ייב של שבתאי או[19] מאדים וזה יודע מהלוחות הנזכרות.
וי שתהיה עם ראש התלי או זנבו[20] או ביניהם פחות מייב
מעלות. זי שתהיה בסוף המזל. חי שתהיה מייט[21] מאזנים[22] עד גי[23]
מעקרב.[24] טי שתהיה[25] ממתנת בהליכתה. עד[26] הנה ענין[27] באור
המלות[28] הנופלות בזה המאמר

---

[1]בכוכב שהוא: בבייח(?) שהוא ‫ו‬ בכוכב שהוא בבית שנאתו כשיהיה במזל נכח ביתו: בכוכבים
שהם בבית שנאתם כשהם במזל שהוא נוכח ביתם **פ**

[2]יקראו: יקרא **א**

[3]מזלות מתהפכים: אלו **ש** signa convertibilia seu mobilia L add.

[4]טלה ומאזנים וסרטן וגדי: טמסייג **פ**

[5]שור ואריה ועקרב ודלי: שעאייד **פ** שור אריה עקרב דלי **ש**

[6]תאומים ובתולה קשת ודגים: תבקייד **פ**

[7]יאמר: ויאמר **ש**

[8]בהליכתו: motu et cursu L

[9]מהלך: מהלכו **ש**

[10]בי: ני **א**

[11]אי שני: ושני אי **ש**

[12]שני: ולצדק אי ולמאדים לייא ללבנה ייג add. **פ**

[13]מהלכו ביום אחד יותר ממהלכו האמצאי: יותר **ופש**

[14]ומהלך: והמהלך **פש**

[15]רעת הלבנה: רעות הלבנה ‫ו‬ רעות ללבנה **פ** ורעת הלבנה בהליכתו **ש**
Mala et impedimenta Lune L

[16]רבים: om. ‫ו‬

[17]בינה: הירח **פ**

[18]שתהיה: שיהיה **פ**

[19]או: של **ש** add.

[20]זנבו: עם **ש** add.

[21]מייט: a gradu .xix. L

[34] ואתחיל בזכרון[1] הכללים הצריכים[2] לפי[3] כונת זה[4] המאמר[5]. אם תרצה להקיז דם השמר שלא תהיה הלבנה במזל תאומים[6] ולא[7] תהיה עם שבתאי או עם מאדים ולא[8] על מבט רביעית[9] או נכח מהם גם[10] לא מכוכב חמה. אמנם מבט שלישית[11] או ששית ממאדים[12] יותר טוב ממבט שלישית[13] או ששית משבתאי. [35] ובכלל השמר[14] שלא תגע בברזל לעשות חבורה[15] באבר מן האברים בזמן שהלבנה באותו מזל[16] המורה[17] על האבר[18] ההוא. [36] דמיון זה אם רצית לעשות חבורה או להקיז מן[19] הראש לא[20] תקיז בעוד הלבנה בטלה[21] שהוא מזל הראש ואם מן הצואר בעוד[22] הלבנה[23] בשור[24] שהוא מזל הצואר[25] וכן כלם. וזה[26] מנוסה ומוסכם מן[27] הראשונים ומן האחרונים. [37] אם תרצה להאכיל או להשקות רפואה לשלשל[28] שים[29] הלבנה במזל שהיא[30] דומה לליחה שתרצה להריקה. [38] דמיון זה אם תרצה[31] להריק[32] האדומה שים הלבנה במזלות[33] האש שהם טאייק ואם[34]

---

[22] מאזנים: ממאזנים ש

[23] גי: tertium gradum L

[24] מעקרב: עקרב פ

[25] שתתחיה: וף om.

[26] עד הנה: זהו ש

[27] ענין: וף om.

[28] המלות: המזלות פש

[1] בזכרון: om. L

[2] הצריכים: בזכרון פ add. ש om.

[3] לפי כונת זה המאמר: in eo L

[4] זה: om. ש

[5] המאמר: Regule huius tractatus add. L om.

[6] תאומים: פי וזה אם(?) יוקז צן הזרוע פ

[7] ולא תהית עם שבתאי או עם מאדים: ולא עם שבתאי או עם מאדים במזל אחד ש

[8] ולא: או ש

[9] רביעית: רביעי ש

[10] גם לא מכוכב חמה: nec sit in aspectu quarte vel opposito Mercurii L

[11] שלישית או ששית: ששית או שלישית ו

[12] ממאדים: אפש om.

[13] שלישית או ששית: ששית או שלישית ו

[14] השמר: השער ש

[15] חבורה: incisionem vel apertionem L

[16] מזל: המזל פש

[17] המורה על: dominante super L

[18]האבר: פש‏ .om

[19]מן הראש לא תקיז בעוד הלבנה בטלה: מהראש השמר שלא תהיה הלבנה במזל טלה ו

[20]לא תקיז: פ‏ .om

[21]בטלה: in signo Arietis L

[22]בעוד הלבנה: בעודה ו

[23]הלבנה: א‏ .om

[24]בשור: במזל שור פ ש‏ז

[25]הצואר: nec facias hoc vel flebotomiam in brachiis dum Luna erit in Geminis
quod est signum brachiorum add. L

[26]וזה מנסה ומוסכם מן הראשונים ומן האחרונים: וזה מנסה מהראשונים והורו [...]
האחרונים ו

[27]מן הראשונים ומן האחרונים: per primos et ultimos magistros in astrologia L

[28]לשלשל: משלשלת ופ

[29]שים: תשים ו

[30]שהיא: שהוא: ו פ‏ .om

[31]תרצה להריק: ו‏ .om

[32]להריק: לשלשל ופש

[33]במזלות האש: in signo igneo seu calido et sicco L

[34]ואם: Et si vis purgare L

השחורה שים הלבנה במזלות העפר[1] חוץ מגדי שהם משור[2]
ומבתולה ואם תרצה להריק הליחה הלבנה שים הלבנה במזלות
המים שהם סעי"ד ואם תרצה להריק[3] הדם כלומר להקיזה[4] שים
הלבנה באחד ממזלות האויר שהם תי"מ[5] דלי [39] ובלבד שתשמור
בזה התנאי[6] ר"ל שלא יהיה הירח במזל האבר בעת[7] שתרצה להקיז
דם מהאבר ההוא. [40] ואם תרצה להריק הליחה[8] הקזה כוללת[9]
יותר[10] מליחה אחת שים הלבנה באחד ממזלות המים. [41] ואם
תשים אותה במזל עקרב השמר שתעבור שלש מעלות מעקרב ואם
תוכל לכוין שלא יביט אליה שום[11] כוכב אז יהיה[12] יותר טוב.
[42] והשמר באיזו[13] הרקה[14] שתכוין שלא תהיה[15] נותנת הלבנה
כחה[16] לאחד מהכוכבים שהם למעלה מן[17] הארץ גם לא בעל
הצומח ידבק בכוכב שהוא[18] על הארץ כי אז יקיא[19] המשקה. [43]
ואם תתן הכח[20] לכוכבים[21] שהם תחת הארץ לא יזיק על מנת שלא
תתן הכח ממבט[22] רע לאחד מן המזיקים ולא לכוכב שהוא שב
אחורנית כי זה יורה גם כן שיקיא[23] המשקה. [44] ואם בהשקותך[24]
המשלשל[25] יביט שבתאי אל הלבנה והוא עולה בגלגל גבהותו
יורה כי[26] לא ישלשל המשקה כהוגן ואם הוא יורד בגלגל גבהותו
יורה על[27] שלשול יותר מדאי. [45] לפי דעת בטלמיוס[28] יצטרך
שתשמור[29] גם כן בהשקותך המשלשל[30] שלא תהיה

---

[1] העפר חוץ מגדי שהם משור ומבתולה: העפר שור בתולה חוץ מגדי **ש**

[2] משור ומבתולה: שור ובתולה **וש**

[3] להריק הדם כלומר להקיזה: flebotomare vel materiam subtilem evacuare **L**

[4] להקיזה: להקיז **פ**

[5] תי"מ דלי: תאומים מאזנים דלי **פש**

[6] התנאי: הקודם בהקזה **ופש** add. predictam in flebotomia **L**

[7] בעת: om. **Lופ**

[8] הליחה: om. **פש L**

[9] כוללת: להריק הרקה כוללת ו **L** add. purgare add.

[10] יותד מליהה אחת: om. **ו**

[11] שום: ופ om.

[12] יהיה: פ om.

[13] באיזו: באיזה **פ**

[14] הרקה: purgatione vel evacuatione **L**

[15] תהיה נותנת: תתן **ופש**

[16] כחה: כח **ש**

[17] מן הארץ: מהארץ **ו**

[18] שהוא: אשר **ו**

[19] יקיא: patiens add. **L**

הלבנה עם צדק[1] או נגה או נותנת הכח להם[2] כי תקצר ותחלש
פעולת המשלשל. [46] אמנם לא הודו לו[3] הבאים אחריו כפי שיעיד[4]
על זה החכם[5] ר׳ אברהם א״ע ולזה[6] דעת ר׳ אברהם[7] לכוין אם
אפשר זה שלא תביט[8] הלבנה אל כוכב.[9]
[47] ואם תרצה[10] לתת משקה להקיא שים הלבנה במזל[11] שור
או[12] תתן כחה לכוכב שהוא[13] במזל[14] שור או לכוכב שהוא למעלה
על[15] הארץ או לכוכב שהוא שב אחורנית. [48] אם תרצה להכניס
העלול[16] איזה[17] שיהיה במרחץ שים הלבנה באחד ממזלות[18]
המים או באיזה מזל שיהיה[19] על מנת שתהיה[20] על מבט אחד מן
הכוכבים[21] הטובים או עם[22] כל מבטי חמה חוץ מן[23] הנכח. [49] עד
כאן מה שנמצא בספרים[24] אשר[25] אצלינו מזאת החכמה מבחירת
העתים לנתינת המשקים[26] והמשלשלים ועשית[27] ההקזות. [50]
ואמנם כפי התחלות[28] החכמה ושרשיה אפשר שימצאו לאלו[29]
העניינים מבחרים אחרים ועתים[30] נכונים[31] ובלתי[32]

---

[20]הכח: om. פ

[21]לכוכבים שהם: לכוכב שהוא ש

[22]ממבט: במבט פ

[23]שיקיא: patiens add. L

[24]בהשקותך: בהשקות ש בהשקותך המשלשל: cum dabis ad bibendum purgam vel ad laxativum L

[25]המשלשל: purgam vel aliquod laxativum L

[26]כי לא: שלא ש

[27]על שלשול: שהוא ישלשל פ ה ישלשל( ) ש על שלשול יותר מדאי: כי לא ישלשל על שלשול מופלג ויותר מדאי ו

[28]בטלמיוס: טלמיס פ

[29]שתשמור: שישמור פ

[30]המשלשל: om. פ

[1]צדק או נגה: נגה או צדק ו

[2]להם: אליהם פ

[3]לו: לו זה ופ לזה ש

[4]שיעיד: שהעיד וש

[5]החכם ר׳ אברהם א״ע: ר׳ אברהם ב׳ עזרא ו אבן עזי פ הראב״ע ש

[6]ולזה: ולכן ו ולזה דעת ר׳ אברהם: ולפי דעת ו׳ עזי פ ולזה הדעת ב״א ש

[7]אברהם: ראוי פ add.

[8]תביט הלבנה אל כוכב: יביט כוכב אל הלבנה פ

[9]כוכב: שום כוכב ו

[10]תרצה לתת: תתן ו

[11]במזל: om. L

[12]או תתן כחה לכוכב שהוא במזל שור: om. ש

[13]שהוא: om. פ

[14]במזל: כמזל ו

[15]על: מן פ מ- וש

נאותים זולת אשר קדם זכרם אלא שאי אפשר לתת כלל[1] בהם[2] כי
אם[3] בידיעת התחלות החכמה ודרכיה[4] ועדין[5] אולי והכתוב למעלה
מספיק אל הכונה.[6]

[51] אמנם ראיתי לחבר לזה[7] מאמרים וכללים קצרים אשר טוב[8]
לרופא שידעם קצתם בהנהגת הרופא עם החולה וקצתם נוגעים
בהקדמת הידיעה במה שיקרה לחולה עם מה שתעזרהו ידיעתו[9]
ברפואה כי כל זה[10] צריך לרופא שידע[11] מזאת[12] החכמה על[13] צד[14]
היותר טוב. [52] אמר בטלמיוס:[15] כאשר היו[16] השביעי ובעליו[17]
נזוקים לעלות[18] תחליף[19] רופאו.[20] ירצה בזה כי הצומח ובעליו
יורה[21] על החולה והשביעי ובעליו יורו על[22] הרופא ולכן כשיוזק[23]
השביעי ובעליו מחבור או[24] מבט מזיק יורו[25] על טעות[26] הרופא
ושבוש ממנו ולכן ראוי[27] להמירו. [53] וזה המאמר אע״פי[28] שהוא
נגד הרופא ראוי הוא[29] שהוא[30] יהיה ידוע אצלו כי[31] אין נקי מן
השגיאות ושגיאות[32] מי יבין ואין ראוי לרופא הטוב

[16]העלול איזה שיהיה: איזה עלול פ העלול ש

[17]איזה שיהיה: om. L

[18]ממזלות: מן המזלות פ

[19]שיהיה: שתהיה פ

[20]שתהיה: שיהיה וש

[21]הכוכבים: om. ש

[22]עם כל: om. ו

[23]מן הנכח: מהנכח ש

[24]בספרים: מן הספרים פ

[25]אשר: הם ו add.

[26]המשקים והמשלשלים: potationes laxativas L

[27]ועשית ההקזות: ולהקאות ולהקזות ו

[28]התחלות החכמה ושרשיה: principia scientie L

[29]לאלו: לאלה פש

[30]ועתים: נאותים ש

[31]נכונים: perfecta L

[32]ובלתי נאותים: inutilia L

[1]כלל: כולל ש generalitatem seu generalem regulam L

[2]בהם: om. ש

[3]אם: om. פ

[4]ודרכיה: et adhuc etiam est difficile L

[5]ועדין אולי: attamen L

[6]הכונה: הנכונה א

[7]לזה מאמרים: זה ממאמרים א אל זה מאמרים ו אל זה המאמרים פ

[8]טוב: multum utiles L

[9]ידיעתו: אל זה הידיעה ו

המכוין להגיע הבריאות אל החולה שבוש וימנע[1] מזה כדי לחוס על
כבודו. [54] אמנם כשיראו[2] אלו האותות יחשוד עצמו[3] על הטעות
מהכרת סבת[4] החולי או מהעלם ממנו דרכי הרפואה ויבקש להחליף
אותו או לשתף[5] עמו[6] אחר ובזה יעשה הישר[7] והטוב ויקנה[8] לו שם
טוב. [55] אני איני יודע איזו סבה יתנו חכמי הרפואה על[9] הימים
אשר[10] יפול בהם הבחראן אם הוציאים הנסיון לבד או סמכו זה
על[11] הקש. אמנם ראיתי רופאים[12] מומחים יבהלו[13] כי יראו[14]
בכראן[15] טוב ושלם ביום[16] שאינו בחראני[17] כפי הרפואה[18] ולא ידעו
לתת סבה[19] לזה. [56] ואנשי[20] זאת החכמה יתנו סבה[21]
באלו[22] העניינים יאמרו[23] כי[24] הסבה באלו[25] הבחראנים הוא היות
הירח[26] בתמונות ידועות ממקומה בתחלת החולי [57] וימשלו[27]
זה[28] למה[29] שיעשה בעל הריב[30] המשכיל עם בעל הריב[31] הסכל[32]
וזה כי[33] הטבע בהתגבר[34] העלה

---

[10] זה צריך: כל מה שצריך ש

[11] שידע: שידעהו פ

[12] מזאת החכמה: om. L

[13] על צד היותר טוב: de bene esse L

[14] צד: הצד פ

[15] בטלמיוס: תלמיוס פ

[16] היו השביעי: יהיה חשביעי פ תחיה השביעית ש

[17] ובעליו: או בעליו פ

[18] לעלות: in egris L om. ש

[19] תחליף רופא: remove medicum ab egro L

[20] רופאו: הרופא ו

[21] יורה: יורו פש

[22] על: om. א

[23] כשיזוק: אם היו נזוקים ו

[24] או מבט: ומבט ו

[25] יורו: יורה פש

[26] טעות הרופא ושבוש ממנו: errorem medici L

[27] ראוי להמירו: debet removeri vel mutari et alium haberi L

[28] אע, פי, אע״פ פש

[29] הוא: om. פ

[30] שהוא יהיה: שיהיה ו

[31] כי אין...הטוב: om. פ

[32] ושגיאות מי יבין: om. L

[1] וימנע מזה כדי לחוס על כבודו: et in hoc vertitur eius honor L

[2] כשיראו: כשיראה ש

[3] עצמו על הטעות מהכרת סבת: מהטעות על הכרת חברת(?) החולי ש

[4] סבת: causas L

[5]לשתף: רופא א add. ש

[6]עמו: vel sine eo add. L

[7]הישר והטוב: quod debet L

[8]ויקנה: ויקרא אפ ויקנה לו שם טוב: om. ש

[9]על: אצל פ

[10]אשר יפול בהם הבחראן: שיפלו בהם הבחרנים פ

[11]על הקש: אל זה הקש ו אל הקש פ אל ההקש ש

[12]רופאים: רופא א

[13]יבהלו: יבהילו ש stare turbatos L

[14]יראו: ירא ש

[15]בכראן: בא בכראן ו בכרן פ פי' ג)(.ול ש

[16]ביום: היום ש

[17]בחראני: בחרני פ בחראן ש

[18]הרפואה: החכמה פ

[19]סבה לזה: הסבה פ סבה בזה ש

[20]ואנשי זאת החכמה: Sed astrologi L

[21]סבה: בזה ש add.

[22]באלו הענינים: לזה בכל זה ו בכל אלה הדברים פש

[23]יאמרו: ויאמרו ש

[24]כי: ש om.

[25]באלו: כי אלו א בכל אלו פ

[26]הירח: om. L

[27]וימשלו: וימשלוהו פ וימשילו ש

[28]זה: זאת ש

[29]למה שיעשה: om. ו

[30]הריב: ש om.

[31]הריב: ש om

[32]הסכל: השכל אפש

Nam sapiens quiescit a litigio cum videt stultum alieno iuvamine
fulcitum, donec cesset id iuvamen add. L

[33]כי: לפי ש add.

[34]בהתגבר: להתגבר פש

עליו בתחלת החולי לא יתנועע להתגבר עליו באותו העת[1] וימתין
חול הירח במקום הפכי לאותו מקום[2] שהיה[3] בו בתחלת החולי כדי[4]
שלא יהיה[5] כח החומר המתנועע בו[6] כפי מה שהיה[7] עליו בתחלת
העלה ואז יתעורר[8] להיות בעל ריבו נצוח[9] [58] וזה[10] בחול הירח
במקום[11] הפכי לו[12] יפלו הבחראנים[13] ויהיו צודקים
ונכונים וטובים או רעים כפי תמונת הירח אל המקום שהיה[14]
בתחלת החולי. [59] וכפי מבטי הכוכבים אליה[15] ולפי שהתקיף
שבמבטים הוא הנכח היה[16] היותר אמתי והיותר צודק
שבבחראנים[17] אם[18] לרע אם לטוב יום י״ד[19] ואז הגיע הירח אל
נכח מקומה [60] כי אם מצאנו הירח בתחלת החולי[20] בראש טלה
הנה היא[21] תגיע אל נכח[22] מקומה[23] ביום י״ד[24] מהחולי. [61]
ונכח[25] מקומה[26] הוא מאזנים אשר[27] הוא הפכי לטלה באיכות
המתפעלת וכן כל נכח אי אפשר שלא יהיה הפכות ביניהם אם
באיכות פועלת ואם[28] באיכות מתפעלת או בשתיהם[29] וזה ברוב.
[62] וכן הוא הענין[30] בהגיע אל מרובע מקומה הוא היום השביעי כי
אז תגיע[31] גם כן אל מקום הפכי למקומה בהתחלת החולי באחת[32]
האיכויות[33] הנזכרות. [63] ולכן יאמרו

---

[1]העת: עת **ש**

[2]מקום: המקום **ש**

[3]שהיה: שהיתה **ו** שיהיה **ש**

[4]כדי שלא יהיה כח החומר המתנועע בו כפי מה שהיה עליו בתחלת העלה: om. L

[5]יהיה: om. **א**

[6]בו: om. **א**

[7]שהיה: שיתנועע **ו**

[8]יתעורר: יתנועע **פ**

[9]נצוח: מנוצח **פ**

[10]וזה: ולזה ו**פש**

[11]במקום: בזה **ו** במזל **פש**

[12]לו: למקומו בתחלת החולי **ו** למקומה בתחלת החולי **פ** למקומו בתחלת **ש**
loco in quo erat in principio egritudinis L

[13]הבחראנים: id est dies cretici add. L

[14]שהיה: שהיתה שם **פ** שהיתה **ש**

[15]אליה: האלה **פ** אליהן **ש**

[16]היה: הוא **ש**

[17]שבבחראנים: om. **ו**

[18]אם לרע אם לטוב: אם לטוב אם לרע **פ** אם אל הטוב אם אל הרע **ש**

[19]י״ד: הי״ד **פש**

[20]החולי: על צד משל **ו** add. על דרך משל **פ** add. עד״מ **ש** add.

[21]היא: om. **פ**

שגבול[1] היום השביעי הוא בהיות הלבנה
על מבט רביעית[2] עם מקומה[3] בתחלת החולי ויום י״ד[4] על מבט נכח
ויום עשרים או יום[5] כ״א על מבט רביעית[6] השנית[7] ויום כ״ז או כ״ח
תשוב[8] אל מקומה בהתחלת[9] החולי. [64] ושאע״פי[10] שלא[11] יהיה
שם הפכיות האיכויות[12] לפעמים[13] יהיה בן גבול[14] טוב כי[15] אחר
שעברו כל המבטים ופעל הפכיות האיכויות[16] ומנע[17] בהתגבר החולי
יחליש[18] כח החומר עד שתהיה החולי בירידה. [65] ובשוב הירח אל
מקומה בתחלת החולי יתנועע הטבע לנצח[19] החולי כמי[20] שיחליף
כח. [66] אמנם שאר ימי הגבולים הנה ינתנו[21] גם כן[22] סבה.
ויאמרו[23] היום החמישי הוא יום הגבול[24] להיותו על מבט ששית
אל[25] מקומה[26] הראשון שהיתה[27] בתחלת החולי. וככה[28] ביום י״א
תהיה על מבט שלישית ממקומה[29] בתחלת החולי. ויום[30] י״ז[31]
כיום[32] י״א ואם[33] כ״ד כיום[34] ה׳.

---

²²נכח: om. ש

²³מקומה: מקומו פ

²⁴יי״ד: היי״ד פ

²⁵ונכח מקומה הוא: שהוא ו

²⁶מקומה: מקומו פ

²⁷אשר הוא: והוא ו פ om.

²⁸ואם באיכות מתפעלת: או מתפעלת ופש

²⁹בשתיהם: בשתיהן פש

³⁰הענין: om. ש

³¹תגיע גם כן: גם כן תגיע ג״כ פ

³²באחת: ואחת פ באחד ש

³³האיכויות: האיכות פ

¹שגבול: שהגבול א terminus seu boaran L

²רביעית: רביעי פ

³מקומה: מקומו ו

⁴יי״ד: היי״ד ש

⁵יום: ו om.

⁶רביעית: רביעי פ

⁷השנית: השני פש

⁸תשוב: ישוב ופש

⁹בהתחלת: בתחלת ופש

¹⁰ושאע״פי: ואז אע״פ ו אע״פ פש

¹¹שלא יהיה: שאין פ

¹²האיכויות: האיכות פש

¹³לפעמים...הפכיות האיכויות: om. ש

¹⁴גבול...עד שתהיה החולי: גבול לכח בחומר עד שיגיע החולי ו

¹⁵כי: או פ

[67] אמנם הגבולים אשר יפלו בשאר הימים[1] הם להיות[2] הלבנה[3]
פעמים מהירה במהלכה[4] ותגיע[5] בד׳ או בו׳ למקום שתגיע בו[6]
כשהיא ממתנת במהלכה[7] בה׳ או[8] בז׳ ולזה יקדם[9] הבחראן בד׳
או בו׳ וכן מי״יא לסוף התשיעי. [68] ופעמים יתאחר מהלכה ותגיע
בראש הטי[10] למקום שתגיע[11] בו[12] פעם אחרת בשביעי. [69] ולזה
יפול הגבול[13] לפעמים ברביעי ובו׳ ובט׳ ובזאת[14] הסבה בעצמה
היא הסבה לשאר הימים אשר יראה בהם הגבול לפעמים[15] בימים
שאינם בחראנים הסמוכים[16] בחראני בעשירי[17] בי״ג[18] ובי״ט[19] וכי[20]
וכי״ח.[21] [70] אמנם הימים אשר אחר[22] כי״ח[23] כבר אמרו הרופאים
שיפול הבחראן בהם[24] מז׳ ימים לז׳ ימים. וזה כי[25] להתישך[26] החולי
לא התגבר הטבע בשוב הירח אל[27] מקומה[28] בתחלת החולי. [71]
ולא[30] יוכל להתעורר עד שוב הירח אל מבט רביעית ממקומה או
נכח[31] כי הם המבטים החזקים. [72] ובכלל בעת היות הירח אל[32]
איזה מבט ממקומה בתחלת[33] החולי יתעורר הטבע להתגבר על
החולי או[34] ינצח או ינוצח כפי מבטי

---

[16]האיכויות: האיכות פ
[17]ומנע בהתגבר החולי: מהתגבר החולי פ
[18]יחליש: יחלש פש debilitatur et minuitur L
[19]לנצח: לנצחי פ ad vitandum L
[20]כמי שיחליף: כמו שיחלוף פ
[21]יתנו: הם יתנו ו יתנו פש dant astrologi L
[22]כן: בהם פש add.
[23]ויאמרו: כי פש add.
[24]הגבול: גבול וש
[25]אל: על א
[26]מקומה: מקומו ו
[27]שהיתה: שהיה ופש
[28]וככה...בתחלת החולי: om. פ
[29]ממקומה: ממקומו ו
[30]ויום י״ז כיום י״א: ואם היום יום י״ז יהיה כחו כיום י״א פ
[31]י״ז: תהיה ש add.
[32]כיום: יהיה כוזב ו
[33]ואם: ויום ושפ et dies L
[34]כיום: ויום ו
[1]הימים: ימים פ
[2]להיות: היות פ
[3]הלבנה: חסרה פ add.
[4]במהלכה: בהליכתה ש
[5]ותגיע: ומגיע ו והגיע פ

---

⁶בו: פעם אחרת ם = add. ו L add. alia vice .om

⁷במהלכה: בהליכתה פש

⁸או בו׳: ובי׳ ם

⁹יקדם: נקדם ם קדם ש

¹⁰הטי: השלישי ם

¹¹שתגיע בו פעם אחרת בשביעי: שהגיע פעם אחרת בשלישי ם שהגיע פעם אחרת בו׳ ש

¹²בו: ו .om

¹³הגבול לפעמים: ם .inv

¹⁴ובזאת הסבה: והסבה הזאת ופש

¹⁵לפעמים: ש .om

¹⁶הסמוכים: מונים ם לימים ו add. ליום ש L add dies

¹⁷בעשירי: בעשירית ו L x. dies est sicut

¹⁸ביי״ג: וי״ג ום ויום יי״ג ש L .xiii.

¹⁹ובי״ט: וי״ח ום וי״ט ש L xix. et

²⁰וכי: ש .om L xx. et

²¹וכי״ח: וכי״ט (ח) ם כי״ח ש L et.xxvii.

²²אחר: L prope

²³כי״ח: הכי״ט (ח) ם הכי״ח ש (in the margin)

²⁴בהם: שבהם ם

²⁵כי: ש .om

²⁶להתישן: ם .om

²⁷אל: על ם ש?

²⁸מקומה: מקומו ו

²⁹החולי: ש .om

³⁰ולא: ולזה א שלא ש

³¹נכח: הנכח ם L add. eius

³²אל: על פש

³³בתחלת החולי יתעורר הטבע להתגבר על החולי: או נכח כי הם המבטים החזקים ובכלל בעת היות הירח ש End MS

³⁴או ינצח: וינצח ום L Et vincit

המצליחים או המזיקים אל הירח ומצבם[1] בגלגל. [73] אנמם אחר
עבור הארבעים[2] לא יראה בחראן ביום ידוע מצד הרפואה לפי
שאינו מוגבל מצד הרפואה. [74] אמנם מצד זאת החכמה[3] לבקי[4]
בה מצד השמש כי דרך הירח בעלות החדות היא[5] דרך השמש
בעלות הישנות עם תנאים אחרים יארך ספורם אין[6] מקום לזכרם
הנה. [75] ובקדחות[7] הבאות בדלוג יהיה יחס מספר ההקפים[8]
כמספר[9] הימים בקדחות תמידיות. [76] אמנם הקדמת הידיעה
בשלמות הגבול ואמתתו והיותו טוב או רע זה יודע[10] וילקח הוראה
עליו כפי מבטי המזיקים[11] או המצליחים אל מקומות הירח הנז' כי
המצליחים יורו על טוב והתגבר[12] הטבע על העלה והמזיקים יורו על
רע[13] אלא אם כן יהיה[14] הפכי לעלה והירח בגבולו כי אז לא יזיק
מבט המזיק. [77] ואע"פי[15] שהדבור בזה כפי הצורך יארך ויקשה[16]
למי[17] שאינו בעל זאת המלאכה[18] עם[19] כל זה אני[20] רוצה להזכיר
כללים מה על זה[21] שתקל ידיעתם [78] ואומר[22] אם הלבנה בהיותה
על[23] מרובע מקומה בתחלת החול‹י›[24] או לנכחו בביתה או בבית
כבודה הוא חצי סימן טוב אע"פי[25] שלא התחבר[26] עם כוכב ולא
יביט אליה. [79] וככה דרך השמש אם יארך החולי והפך הדבר אם
היו[27] בבית שפלותם או[28] שנאתם. [80] אם

---

[1]ומצבם: status vel situs eorum L

[2]הארבעים: dies add. L

[3]החכמה: יודע פ add. L sciri

[4]לבקי בה: per scientem dies terminorum L יום הגבול ופ add.

[5]היא: הוא פ

[6]אין: כי אין ו אינן פ

[7]ובקדחות: וק בקדחות פ

[8]ההקפים: הרקפים( ) פ

[9]כמספר: במספר פ

[10]יודע ו-: om. L

[11]המזיקים או המצליחים: ופ inv.
planetarum bonorum vel dampnosorum L

[12]והתגבר: conari (?) et dominari L והתגבר הטבע על העלה: ו om.

[13]רע: malum vel dampnum L

[14]יהיה: המזיק ופ

[15]ואע"פי: ואע"פ פ

[16]ויקשה: et aliquantulum durum L

[17]למי שאינו בעל זאת המלאכה: אלא למי שהוא בעל זאת החכמה פ nescienti L

[18]המלאכה: החכמה ו

[19]עם כל זה אני רוצה להזכיר: את כל זאת אני רואה והזכיר פ

הלבנה בתחלת החולי בלי[1] מבט וביום[2] הגבול יביט אליה כוכב
טוב או רע יתחדש על[3] החולה דבר טוב או רע
כפי תולדת הכוכב שלא עלה על לב. [81] אם הלבנה נקדרת
בהיותה על מרובע מקומה בתחלת[4] החולי או הנכח הוא סימן רע
כפי[5] הקדרות. [82] אם המזל הצומח בתחלת החולי ראש טלה או
מאזנים והלבנה באחת[6] היתדות הנה[7] הגבולים יהיו נאמנים בלא[8]
ספק בהגיע הלבנה אל המרובע או הנכח. [83] אם הלבנה[9] בתחלת
החולי במזל מתהפך יורה על מהירות דברי[10] החולה בין טוב ובין
רע ואם במזל עומד יתארך החולי ואם במזל שני[11] גופות יצא מחולי
אל חולי. [84] אם היה סבת החולי תוספת[12] בגוף ואור[13] הלבנה
יוסיף הוא דבר קשה[14] ואם אורה יחסר הוא יותר טוב. [85] ואם[15]
סבת החולי מחסרון[16] ואורה חסר הוא דבר קשה ואם[17] יוסיף
הוא יותר טוב. [86] אם היתה הלבנה בתחלת החולי במזל שהוא
בתולדת הליחה שהולידה החולי הדבר קשה [87] ואם היתה במזל
הפך החולי הוא[18] סימן טוב וכל זה אם לא תתחבר עם כוכב או לא
תביט אליו כי אם יהיה כן יהיה המשפט כפי המבט או המחברת.
[88] מחברת הלבנה עם שבתאי יורה על רע ואורך החולי ובפרט
כשיחסר אורה. [89] אמנם כשהיא[19] בתוספת אורה מעט יזיק
שבתאי ימתין[20] במהלכו יוסיף רע ואם מהיר יחסר. [90] ואם הוא
נזור וקודם נכח השמש אחר שיתרפא ישוב לחליו. [91] אם שבתאי
במקום גבהותו או קרוב ממנו והחולי[21] יש בו עצור יוסיף רע על
רע. ואם בשפלותו יחסר[22] מרעתו ואם החולי יש בו שלשול והוא
בשפלותו יוסיף רעה[23] על רעה ובגבהותו[24] יחסר מרעתו. [92] אם
הלבנה עם צדק[25] או על מבטו מבט[26] ששית ושלישית
סימן טוב

---

[20]אני רוצה: רואה אני ו

[21]זה: זאת פ

[22]ואומר: Primo dico L

[23]על מרובע: ברובע ו

[24]החולי...: החול פ om. א

[25]אעי״פי: אעי״פ פ

[26]התחבר: תתחבר ופ

[27]היו: היה א Luna vel Sol L

[28]או: בבית פ .add

[1]בלי: בלא ו לה פ

[2]וביום הגבול: i.e. diei cretici add. L

[3]על: אל פ

[4]בתחלת: לתחלת ו

מאד ויותר למי שעבר חצי ימיו וכן מבט נכח או מרובע יורה על
טוב רק שיבוא ביגיעה.[1] [93] זה[2] מה שרציתי לכללו בזה המאמר
שהוא נקל לכל רופא משכיל ובעל[3] לב לדעתו אם ירצה להשתמש
בו והוא צודק ברוב כפי שהעידו[4] חכמי הנסיון [94] ואם לפעמים
יחטא לא יפלא על זה כי הרבה פעמים יקרה זה אם מצד הוראות
מולד החולה אשר הם בלתי מסכימות להוראות הנלקחות מעתות
החולי והבחראן ואותן הוראות המולד הן העקר אם מצד התשובה
ומעשים טובים המקרעים גזר דין[5] ואם מצד העלם כל שרשי
החכמה[6] הזאת מהרופא אשר אי אפשר לכללם בקצור בזה המאמר.
[95] והכל לאל יתי רופא כל בשר ומפליא לעשות אין עוד מלבדו[7]
תם תם תם.

---

[5]כפי הקדרות: secundum modum eclipsis L

[6]באחת: באחד פ

[7]הנה: פ om.

[8]בלא: בלי ופ

[9]הלבנה: causa L

[10]דברי: om. L

[11]שני: משני ו

[12]תוספת: humorum add. L

[13]ואור הלבנה יוסיף: והלבנה תוסיף אורה פ

[14]קשה: valde durum L

[15]ואם סבת החולי...הוא יותר טוב: וההפך בהפך פ

[16]מחסדון: חסדון ו

[17]ואם: אורה ו add.

[18]הוא סימן טוב: יהיה סימן טוב ו הדבר טוב פ

[19]כשהיא: כשהוא פ כשהוא בתוספת אורה: כשיוסיף ו

[20]ימתין במהלכו: ממתין בהליכתו פ ואם שבתי ממתין בהליכתו ו
Et si Saturnus est tardus L

[21]והחולי יש בו עצור: et eger est constipatus L

[22]יחסר: יחלש ו יחסר מרעתו ואם החולי יש בו שלשול והוא בשפלותו: om. א
minuetur malum. Et si eger est laxus, et Saturnus est in suo descensu L

[23]רעה על רעה: רע על רע ו ברעתו פ

[24]ובגבהותו: ואם בגבהותו ו ובגהותו א

[25]צדק: הצדק פ

[26]מבט: om. L

[1]ביגיעה: ביגיע פ פגיעה לחולה ו egri add. L

[2]זה מה שרציתי...תם תם תם: והבטח בייי חסד יסובבנו תם ונשלם תהלה לאל עולם נשלם
יום לבנה שעת שבתאי ועם כל זה עזרי יהיה מעם השם פ

[3]ובעל לב: om. L

[4]שהעידו: מה שהעידו ו om. L

[5]דין: דינו ו

[6]החכמה הזאת: זאת החכמה ו

[7]מלבדו: qui vivit et regnat in secula seculorum, amen add. L

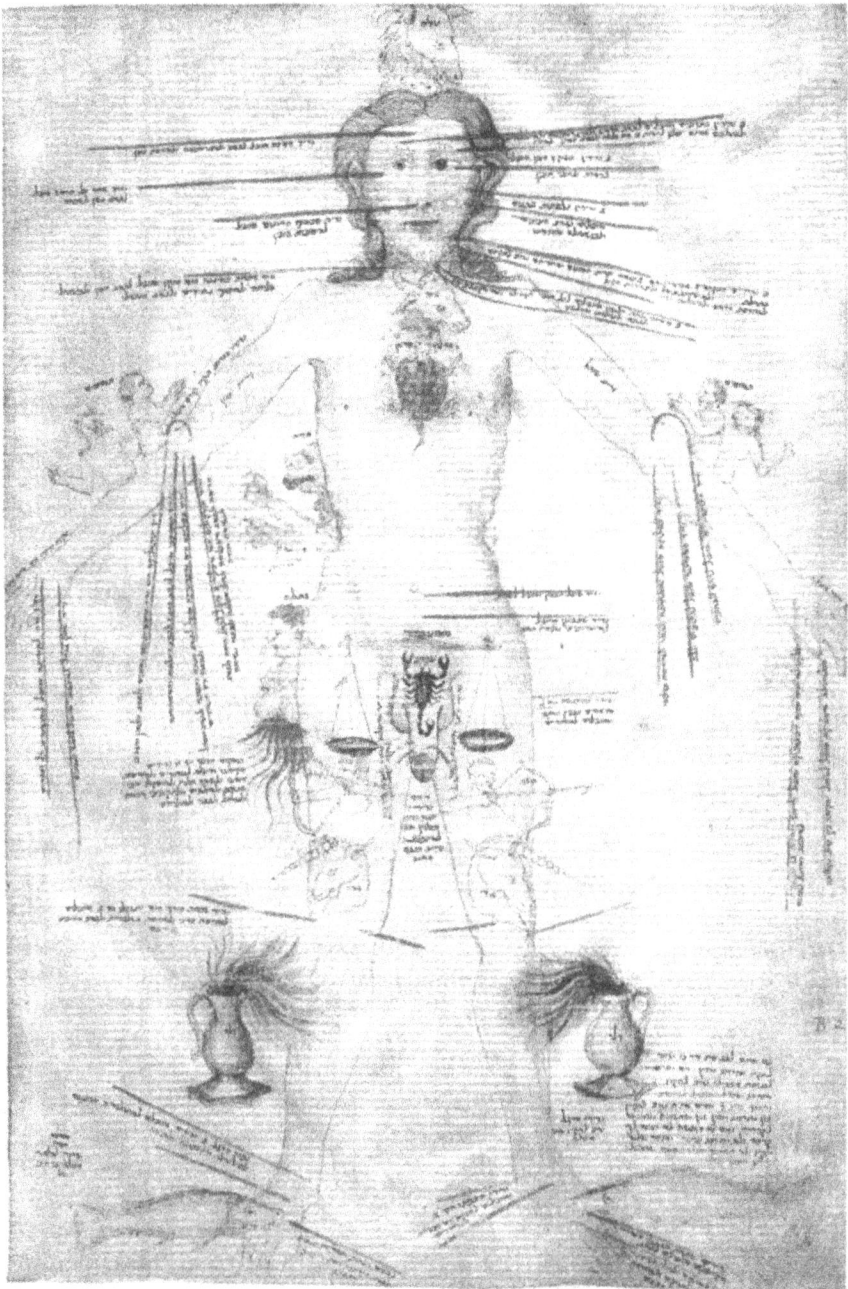

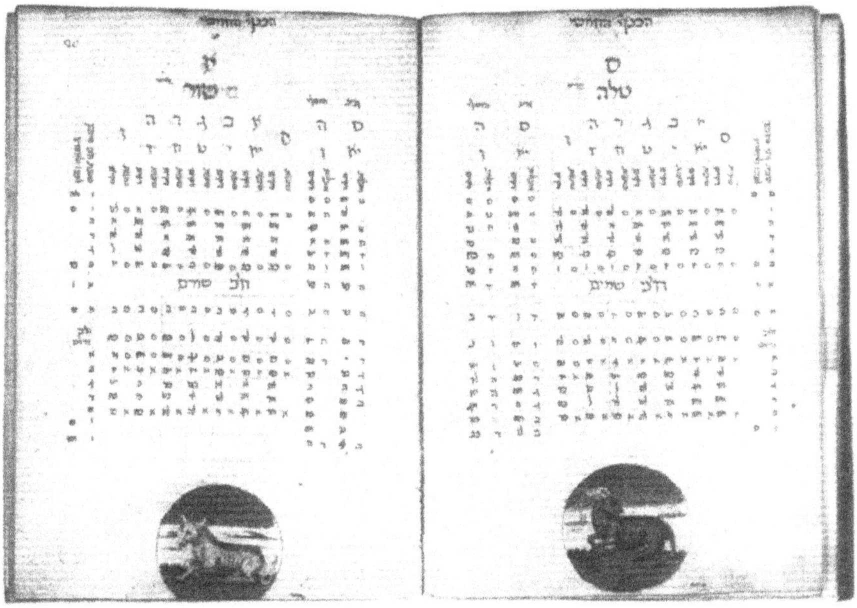

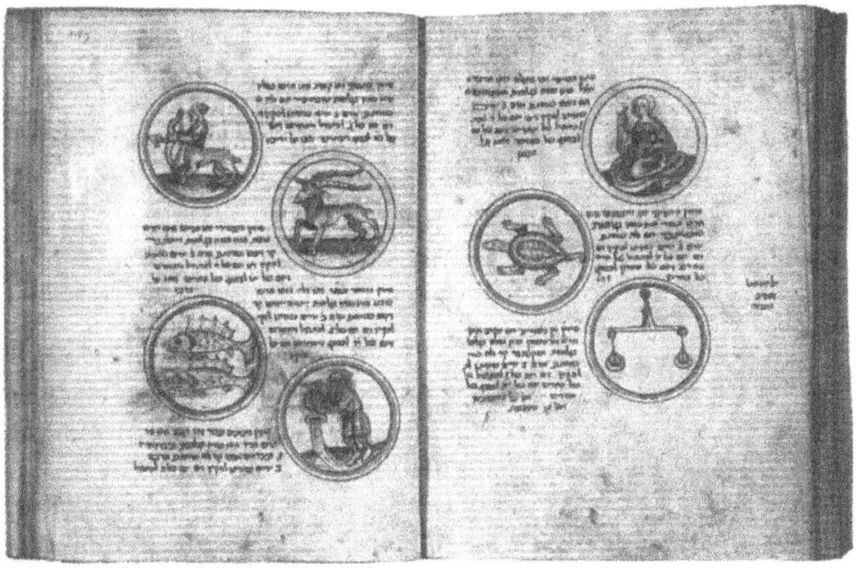

Chapter Three

The Latin Text

Edited by Charles Burnett

T he Latin version of David's work on astrological medicine is
found in a single manuscript: Barcelona, Biblioteca de Catalunya
634, fols. 84r–90r. This manuscript was written in the first half of
the fifteenth century (before 1446), evidently in Barcelona (there are
annotations in Catalan), and consists of a collection of Latin texts on
astronomy and astrology. Several of these texts have Jewish connections, and among them is a large portion of the earliest known Latin
version of Abraham bar Ḥiyya's *Tsurat ha-Aretz* ("On the Form of
the Earth").[1] David's treatise is simply headed "Tractatus Davidis
Iudei" ("The Treatise of David the Jew") and consists of a continuous text followed by tables. The tables are missing in the Hebrew
version, but are referred to several times in the text and are clearly
meant to accompany it, as they do in the Latin version. They give,
in a convenient tabular manner, the houses (*domus*) and exaltations
(*honores*) of the planets as well as their falls (*vilia*) and detriments
(*malivolentiae*) and the degrees of their nodes (*caput* and *infernum caput draconis*), apogees and perigees (*altitudo* and *bisextus*); the lords
of the triplicities, the terms (*termini*),[2] the decans (*facies*), the ninth-
parts (*novenae*), and the twelfth-parts (*virtutes duodecimae*);[3] and the
characteristics of each of the planets and the signs of the zodiac,
especially in regard to the parts of the body and the diseases they
signify. All of this information comes ultimately from Abraham
Ibn Ezra's *Reshit Ḥokhmah* (*Principium sapientiae*).[4] Although the astrological terminology largely corresponds to that used in Petrus
d'Abano's Latin version, printed by Peter Liechtenstein in Venice in
1507, it is possible that the Latin tables have been translated directly
from Hebrew tables already dependent on Ibn Ezra's work.

After the tables there is a short paragraph written in the same
hand concerning the planets' operation over minerals and plants,

citing "Aristotle's *De secretis*." Since this is not the *Secreta secretorum* of Pseudo-Aristotle, it could be another Hebrew work. However, its relevance to the text of David Judaeus medicus is less obvious.

Passages differing from those in the Hebrew are in italics; the frequent instances of alternative translations of a single Hebrew term (doublets) are not indicated. The scribe follows the Spanish practice of writing single consonants and no "h," e.g., "*aduc, atamen, aplicare, dificile, sagitarius, suficit*" (but contrast "*occulus*"). Also, "n" is always omitted in "*demostra-*" and usually omitted in "*dapnos-*" (for classical "*damnos-*"). In the edition classical Latin orthography has been restored, except in the cases of "e" for "ae," "mpn" for "mn," and "ch" in "michi" and "nichil" (which alternates with "nil").

Note the following technical terms (I am not sure of the reading of some of them):

boaran: crisis
sistrenum tabularum: a set of tables (the reference is to the
   tables following the text)
conari: to prevail (of a disease).
conatus: strength (of a disease)
antiquatus: chronic
antiquatio: chronicity
saltando: intermittent
cavilla: cardine

In the tables, further vernacular and unusual terms appear: the body-parts *melsa* for spleen, *dura* for liver, *torela* for a woman's privy parts (?), and the diseases *porcellane, gracella*, and *bamboles*.

/f. 84r/Tractatus Davidis Iudei.

[1] Quia, *ut dicit Tolomeus in Centiloquio*, vultus huius seculi sunt vultibus celestibus similes,[5] et ab illis recipiunt omne signum quod in eis est et omnem transmutationem que in eis fit, quecumque sit illa, et scientia stellarum—hoc est pars experimentalis illius—tractat de casibus in quibus cadit transmutatio in hoc mundo elementorum virtute celesti (est enim transmutatio motus de sanitate in egritudinem et econtra) et practica scientie medicine tractat de hac transmutatione in qua sepe deveniunt corpora, ergo sequitur quod est proportio et societas inter has duas artes, scilicet inter practicam medicine et partem scientie stellarum predictam.

[2] Et sicut de perfectione astrologi est scire in arte medicine et in natura hominum et etiam res medicinales, ut per illas possit virtutes celestes iuvare et patientes disponere ad recipiendum operationem agentium, et etiam ad vitandum multa ab operatione agentium cum facere voluerit, [3] sic est de perfectione medici quod sciat in virtutibus celestibus et inde servire in hominibus, ut sciat disponere agentia procul et prope ad operandum in patientibus, et quod patientes sint ad hec dispositi, et cum hoc quod etiam sciat et possit prenoscitare in diebus creticis bonos dies et malos, plus quam sciat arte sua, nec in hoc debet sciens dubitare nec etiam secularis.

[4] Attamen quia vita hominis est brevis et quelibet harum artium est *multum* prolixa, nec habet perfectionem nec earum finis potest attingi vel haberi *nisi cum multis laboribus et periculis*, et nullus hominum sufficeret ad comprehendendum perfectiones illas particulas, multo minus est possibile ut vita unius hominis sufficiat ad veniendum ad finem ambarum scientiarum, [5] premaxime quia corda hominum sunt debilitata, [6] ideo est homini utilius quod sit dominus unius scientie tantum quam si sciret modicum de una et modicum de alia. Et propterea raro accidit quod inveniatur medicus qui sit astrologus vel sciens in scientia stellarum, licet sit necessaria in medicina. [7] Et ideo medici interdum vadunt ad illos quos credunt scire in scientia stellarum et *eorum dicto vel consilio* se regunt in electione temporum ad faciendum opera sua.

[8] Et ob hoc quidam notabilis amicus meus rogavit me quem cogitavit *aliquid sentire in dicta scientia*, ut componerem unum tractatum parvum de hiis que indiget medicus totidie in dando laxativa, ciropes et vomitiva, et in faciendo flebotomias, *quia in talibus indiget scientia stellarum*. Et quia ista frequenter accidunt, est necessarium habere respectum magnum et deliberationem ad ea faciendum, ut eius opera habeant et perveniant ad bonam perfectionem. [9–10] *Et propterea volens ei obedire iuxta mee scientie paucitatem*, composui hunc tractatum parvum secundum quod abstraxi a libris de hoc compilatis, nil a me innovando, et hoc Deo michi auxiliante, *sine quo factum est nichil*.

/f. 84v/[11] Sciendum quod quilibet volens se iuvare huiusmodi tractatu habet necesse scire computare loca .vii. planetarum cotidie de almenach. [12] Quod scire est multum facile etiam nil scienti *in scientia astrologie*, [13] et specialiter de quinque planetis—videlicet Saturno, Iove, Marte et Sole et Mercurio—nam loca horum computare *cum almanaco* est multum breve et facile. [14] Sed compotum Veneris et Lune est difficile et turbatum modicum illi qui non habet in usu. Ideo est necesse uti computare illud volenti habere compotum verum, [15] vel saltem quod iam teneat locum ipsorum planetarum computatum inde plures dies et annos per illos qui id computare sciunt. [16] Pari modo est necesse habere secum sistrenum tabularum quod poni solet in fine almanachii, quem sistrenum abstraxerunt sapientes in iudicio per modum abbreviationis a libris scientie astrologie, et per quem sciunt breviter et faciliter naturas signorum et stellarum et domos eorum, et ipsorum altitudinem et profunditatem, honorem et malivolentiam, verecundiam et triplicitatem, et eorum terminum et faciem, et alia que necessaria sunt in hoc tractatu.

[17] Et quia dictum sistrenum tabularum non omnes habent, ideo deliberavi eligere ex illis tabulis quod necessarium est in hoc tractatu ad intentionem ipsius, [18] et valde modicum est in hiis que elegi quod non sit necessarium in ipso. Et adiunxi dictum sistrenum[6] cum hoc tractatu ne, habens hunc tractatum, habeat dictum sistrenum alibi perquirere, nec etiam indigeat nisi scire loca planetarum uno de duobus modis predictis, [19] et postquam sciunt planetarum loca et alia necessaria scire secundum intentionem huius tractatus, ipsemet poterit per se iuvare in electione temporum convenientium flebotomiis, purgationibus, *laxativis* et vomitivis absque auxilio vel consilio *alicuius*.

[20][7] Postquam preposui que sunt necessaria scire volenti uti huiusmodi tractatu et ad eius intentionem, declarabo quedam vocabula in ipso tractatu posita de quibus sibi serviunt scientes in hac scientia. [21] Dicitur enim quod una stella est cum alia vel unum (sic) planeta cum alio quando est cum ea vel eo in eodem signo, et quod quilibet seu uterque sit in virtute corporis alicuius. Et virtutem corporis cuiuslibet planetarum invenies in tabulis supradictis.[8] [22] Item aspectus quarti est quando unus planeta distat ab alio .xc. gradibus, et aspectus oppositi dicitur quando unus ab alio distat .clxxx. gradibus, et aspectus tertii est quando inter se distant .cxx. gradibus, et aspectus sexti est quando distant .lx. gradibus. [23] Et omnes isti aspectus habent virtutem aspecti (sic), etiam si deficeret de eorum aspectu sex gradus vel minus, et hoc sive ante sive retro. [24] Nam si inter unum planetam et alium sint .xcvi. gradus vel .lxxxiiii., dicitur aspectus quarti. Non tamen est ita fortis sicut quando est aspectus completus, et per hunc modum considera alios aspectus. [25] Item dicitur quod planeta dat virtutem quando est in domo sua vel sui honoris vel triplicitatis, vel in suo termino vel facie, et quod coniungatur cum alio planeta, vel eum inspiciat. Et domos eorum, honorem et triplicitatem, terminumque et faciem scies per tabulas supradictas.

[26] Ascendens vocatur signum quod ascendit in orientem in/ f.-85r/qualibet hora, et potest sciri leviter per instrumenta vel per tabulas, vel grosso modo per horas diei, addendo super gradus Solis unum signum pro quibuslibet duabus horis transactis ab ortu Solis. Hoc tamen licet sit proximum *veritati*, non est mere verum, quia impossibile est ad meram veritatem sine tabulis vel instrumentis pervenire.

[27] Dominus ascendentis dicitur planeta qui est dominus signi ascendentis. Planeta quando est retrogradans habet sciri per hoc almanach. Planeta qui ascendit in circulo sue altitudinis vel descendit in eodem scies per hunc modum. Nam gradum altitudinis scies per tabulas supradictas. [28] Et quando planeta erit ante gradum altitudinis minus de .xc. gradibus vocatur ascendens, et quando est post gradum altitudinis minus de .xc. gradibus vocatur descendens. Gradus autem descensus sive bisextus est oppositum (sic) gradus altitudinis.

[29] Planete boni vel benefortunati sunt Iupiter, Venus et Sol, et etiam Luna quando non habet aliquod de malis vel impedimentis subscriptis. Item, licet Iupiter, Venus et Sol sint communiter boni, potest fieri quod eorum virtus *interdum aliquantulum* debilitetur. Mali vero planete et dampnosi sunt Saturnus et Mars, et Mercurius communiter est dampnosus. [30] Domus septima dicitur signum quod est oppositum signi ascendentis. Planetam esse in domo sui malivoli est quando est in signo opposito domui sue. [31] Signa convertibilia seu mobilia, *id est in quibus unum tempus convertitur in aliud*, sunt Aries, Libra, Carcer (sic) et Capricornus. Signa stabilia sunt Taurus, Leo, Scorpius et Aquarius. Signa media seu duorum corporum sunt Geminis (sic), Virgo, Sagittarius et Piscis.

[32] Planetam esse tardum in suo motu vel cursu est quando vadit in uno die minus suo motu medio, qui est in Saturno duo minuta et .1. segondo (sic). Et dicitur velox quando vadit plus quam motus medius. Et cursus medius Lune est .xiii. gradus et .x. minuta. [33][9] Mala et impedimenta Lune sunt multiplicia. Primum est quod eclipsetur. Secundum quod sit prope Solem minus quam .xii. gradus eundo versus eum vel recedendo ab eo. Tertium quod inter Lunam et gradum oppositi sint minus quam .xii. gradus ante vel retro. Quartum quod sit cum planetis malis seu dampnosis in coniunctione vel aspectu. Quintum quod sit cum virtute duodecima Saturni vel Martis et hoc scies per tabulas supradictas. Sextum quod sit cum Capite Draconis vel Cauda eius, vel quod inter eos sit minus .xii. gradibus. Septimum quod sit in fine signi. Octavum quod sit a gradu .xix. Libre usque ad tertium gradum Scorpionis. Nonum quod sit tarda in suo cursu. Et usque hic est declaratio vocabulorum intervenientium in hoc tractatu.

[34] Nunc incipiam eius intentionem et regulas in eo neces-sarias ponere.

/f. 85v/ Regule huius tractatus

Si vis flebotomari vel febotomiam (sic) facere, cave ne Luna sit in signo Geminis (sic) nec sit cum Saturno et Marte, nec sit in aspectu quarto, nec in opposito eorum, nec sit in aspectu quarte vel opposito Mercurii. Tamen aspectus tertii vel sexti Martis est melior quam aspectus tertii vel sexti Saturni. [35] Et generaliter cave quod non tangas cum ferro aliquod membrum, faciendo incisionem vel apertionem, dum Luna sit in signo dominante super illo membro. [36] Verbi gratia, si vis incisionem vel apertionem facere in capite alicuius, non facias hoc dum Luna erit in signo Arietis quod est signum capitis, nec hoc facias in collo dum Luna erit in Tauro quod est signum colli, *nec facias hoc vel flebotomiam in brachiis dum Luna erit-in Geminis quod est signum brachiorum*, et sic de aliis. Et hoc est probatum et experimentatum per primos et ultimos magistros in astrologia.

[37] Si vis dare potationem vel comestionem aliquam laxati-vam, expecta quod Luna sit in signo simili illi humori quem vis purgare vel evacuare. [38] Ut si vis purgare coleram, fac quod Luna sit in signo igneo *seu calido et sicco*, sicut est Aries, Leo, Sagittarius. Et si vis purgare malencoliam (sic), sit Luna in signo terrestri, qui sunt Taurus, Virgo, excepto tamen Capricorno. Et si vis purgare fleumam, sit Luna in signo aque, ut est Cancer, Scorpius et Piscis. Et si vis flebotomare vel *materiam subtilem* evacuare, sit Luna in ali-quo signo aeris, scilicet Geminis (sic), Libra, Aquarii (sic). [39] Serva tamen condicionem predictam in flebotomia, scilicet quod Luna non sit in signo illius membri a quo vis sanguinem minuere. [40] Si vis facere evacuationem generalem—id est purgare plus quam unum humorem—specta quod Luna sit in uno signorum aque. [41] Et si est in signo Scorpionis, aspice quod transiverunt tres gradus Scorpionis. Et si potes facere quod nullus planetarum habeat aspec-tum cum Luna, melius erit.

[42] Et cave in quacumque purgatione vel evacuatione quod facias per modum quod Luna non det virtutem suam alicui plan-etarum qui sit super terram, nec dominus ascendentis habeat co-niunctionem cum aliquo planetarum qui sit super terram, quia si hoc haberet, vomitaret *patiens* purgam. [43] Et si Luna dat virtutem suam planetis qui sint sub terra, non nocet, dum tamen non det vir-tutem mali aspectus planete dampnoso vel retrogradanti, quia tunc

etiam *patiens* vomitaret purgam. [44] Et si cum dabis ad bibendum purgam vel aliquod laxativum, Saturnus ascendens in circulo sue altitudinis aspiciet Lunam vel habebit aspectum ad eam, significat quod purga non faciet operationem quam deberet. Et si descendit in circulo sue altitudinis, significat evacuationem superfluam. [45] Secundum opinionem Tolomei est etiam necessarium quod caveas quando dabis potationem laxativam ne Luna sit cum Iove nec cum Venere, nec det eis virtutem, quia debilitaret et minueret opera laxativi. [46] Tamen Moderni hoc non concedunt, ut dicit Rabi Abraam Aben Esdra, sed intentio eius est respicere si fieri potest quod Luna non habeat aspectum cum Mercurio.

[47] Si vis dare potationem vomitativam, fac quod Luna sit in Tauro, vel quod det suam virtutem alicui planete qui sit in signo Tauri, vel sit super terram, vel sit retrogra-/f. 86r/-dans. [48] Et si vis quod infirmus intret balneum, expecta quod Luna sit in aliquo signo aque, vel in quovis alio signo, dum tamen habeat aspectum ad aliquem bonum planetam, vel cum quovis aspectu Solis, dum tamen non in opposito.

[49] Usque huc est quod reperimus in libris huius scientie de electione temporum pro dando potationes laxativas et faciendo flebotomias, [50] licet secundum principia scientie sit possibile invenire in hiis alias electiones et tempora perfecta et inutilia ultra ea que nominavimus. Sed impossibile est dare generalitatem seu generalem regulam de hiis nisi sciendo principia scientie *et adhuc etiam est difficile*. Attamen quod supradiximus sufficit ad intentionem.

[51] Deliberavi tamen applicare huic tractatui quedam dicta et regulas breves, multum utiles medico ut eas sciat, que partim tangunt in regimine medici cum infirmo, et partim tangunt in prenosticatione accidentium infirmi, cum hoc quod adiuvabit eum scientia medicine, quia totum hoc est necessarium medico, vel saltem scire debet de bene esse.

[52] Dicit Tolomeus (supra: in Centiloquio .57.): cum septimum et eius dominus in egris fuerint impediti, remove medicum ab egro, quasi velit dicere quia ascendens et eius dominus significant super egrum et septimum et eius dominus significant super medicum. Ideo quando septimum et eius dominus sunt dampnificati per coniunctionem vel per aspectum dampnosum, significat errorem medici; ideo debet removeri vel mutari *et alium haberi*. [53] Et hoc dictum licet sit medico contrarium, tamen ipse hoc scire debet, quia nemo se potest ab erratis excusare, et non est boni medici qui tractat de sanitate infirmi errare, et in hoc vertitur eius honor. [54] Unde,

cum videbit hec signa, dubitabit in se ne erret in cognoscendo causas infirmitatis vel quod vie medicine sint ei occulte. Et ipsemet debet requirere quod patiens habeat alium medicum cum eo *vel sine eo,* et sic faciet quod debet, et consequetur famam bonam.

[55] Nescio quam rationem dant a<u>ctores medicine super diebus creticis in quibus cadit boaran, si hoc habuerunt ex experimento *solum* vel per rationem. Vidi tamen sollemnes medicos stare turbatos quando vident venire boaran bonum et perfectum in die in quo non est boaran secundum scientiam medicine, et causam nesciunt assignare. [56] Sed astrologi dant hiis causam, dicentes quod causa horum boaran est esse in dispositionibus certis de loco in quo erat in principio egritudinis. [57] Et dant exemplum de hoc quod facit sapiens litigans cum stulto. *Nam sapiens quiescit a litigio cum videt stultum alieno iuvamine fulcitum, donec cesset illud iuvamen.* Sic cum infirmitas conatur super naturam in principio egritudinis. Nam non se movet ad faciendum contrarium in illo tempore. Sed expectat quod Luna sit in loco contrarianti illi loco in quo erat in principio egritudinis, et quod virtus materie que movetur in eo non sit in casu in quo erat in principio egritudinis, et tunc movetur natura, eo quod eius adversarius est devictus. [58] Et propterea, quando Luna est in loco contrariante loco in quo erat in principio egritudinis, cadunt boaran, *id est dies cretici,* et/f. 86v/sunt iusti et firmi et boni vel mali secundum figuram Lune loco in quo erat in principio egritudinis, [59] et secundum aspectum planetarum ad Lunam. Et propter hoc quia fortior aspectus est oppositum, ideo verior et iustior boaran in bono vel malo est dies .xiiii., et tunc est Luna perventa ad oppositum sui loci. [60] Quia, si invenimus Lunam in principio egritudinis in capite Arietis, erit in contrario loco in .xiiii. die egritudinis. [61] Et locus contrarius est Libra que contrariatur Arieti in qualitate passiva. Et consimili modo est omne oppositum, quia impossibile est quin sit contrarietas inter ea in qualitate activa vel passiva vel in utraque ut plerumque. [62] Et consimiliter quando Luna pervenit in quadrato sui loci, est dies .vii., quia tunc etiam pervenit ad locum contrariantem loco principii egritudinis in aliqua qualitatum predictarum. [63] Et propter hoc dicunt quod terminus seu boaran diei .vii. est, ideo quia Luna est in aspectu quarto cum suo loco in principio egritudinis. Et dies .xiiii. est in aspectu opposito vel oppositionis, et dies .xx. vel .xxi. est in-aspectu quarto secundo, et dies .xxvii. vel .xxviii. revertitur ad locum suum in principio egritudinis. [64] Et tunc, licet non sit contrarietas qualitatum, aliquando evenit terminus bonus sive boaran bonum, quia postquam omnes aspectus sunt preteriti et contrarietas qualitatum operata est et vetavit

quod egritudo [non] habuit conatum, debilitatur et minuitur virtus materie in tantum quod egritudo est in declinatione. [65] Et quando Luna est reversa ad locum principii egritudinis, natura movetur ad vitandum egritudinem, sicut ille qui recuperat virtutem. [66] Attamen aliis diebus de boaran dant astrologi etiam rationem, dicentes quod dies quintus est dies creticus eo quia Luna est in aspectu sexto loco primo in quo erat in principio egritudinis. Et simile in .xi. die est in aspectu tertio loci principii egritudinis. Et dies .xvii. est sicut .xi. et dies .xxiiii. est sicut quintus.

[67] Attamen termini qui cadunt in aliis diebus sunt ex eo quia Luna interdum est velox in suo cursu et pervenit in quarto vel in sexto ad locum in quo pervenerat *alia vice* quando est tarda in suo cursu in quinto vel in septimo. Et propterea anticipatur boaran in quarto vel sexto, et pari modo de undecimo in fine noni. [68] Et interdum tardatur in suo cursu et pervenit in principio noni ad locum in quo pervenit alia vice in septimo. [69] Et ideo cadit boaran aliquando in quarto et in sexto et in nono, et hec eadem causa est causa aliorum dierum in quibus demonstratur terminus aliquando in diebus qui non sunt boaran sed sunt prope dies boaran, sicut est dies .x., .xiii. et .xix. et .xx. et .xxvii<i>. [70] Attamen dies qui sunt prope[10] .xxviii. iam dicunt medici quod cadit boaran in istis de .vii. in .vii. diebus. Et hoc est quia per antiquationem (sic) egritudinis natura non fuit conata quando Luna reversa est ad locum suum in principio egritudinis. [71] Et non potest moveri donec Luna sit reversa ad aspectum quartum sui loci vel ad oppositum eius, quia hii sunt aspectus fortes. [72] Et generaliter cum Luna est in aliquo aspectu sui loci in principio egritudinis natura movetur ad dominandum super egritudinem. Et vincit vel vincitur secundum aspectus planetarum bonorum vel malorum/f. 87r/ad Lunam et status vel situs eorum in circulo. [73] Attamen post .xl. dies non demonstratur aliquis boaran in die certo per artem medicine, quia non est determinatum per scientiam medicine. [74] Tamen per hanc scientiam sciri potest per scientem dies termini per Solem, quia cursus Lune in egritudinibus acutis est iter Solis [vero] in egritudinibus antiquatis cum aliis condicionibus quas longum esset numerare, et non est hic ponendus locus. [75] Et in febribus que veniunt saltando erit <pro>portio numeri revolutionum[11] sicut numerus dierum in febribus continuis.

[76] Sed tamen prenosticare in perfectione termini et in sui verificatione et in suo esse bono vel malo capitur super hoc demonstratio secundum aspectus planetarum bonorum vel dampnosorum ad loca Lune predicta, quia boni planete significant bonum et quod na-

tura debet conari et dominari super egritudinem, et planete dampnosi significant malum vel dampnum, nisi sit contrarius egritudini, et quod Luna sit in suo termino, quia tunc non nocet aspectus
planete dampnosi. [77] Sed loqui de hoc ut esset necesse sit longum
et aliquantulum durum nescienti, tamen cum toto hoc volo hic dicere super hoc aliquas regulas que faciles sunt ad sciendum.

[78][12] *Primo* dico quod si Luna quando est in quadrato sui loci
in principio egritudinis vel in suo opposito erit in domo sua, vel in
domo sui honoris, est semibonum signum, licet non habeat coniunctionem cum Mercurio, nec aspectus cum illo. [79] Et per hunc modum est cursus Solis si egritudo elongatur. Et est contrarium huius si
sunt Luna vel Sol in domo sui dedecoris vel sui malivoli. [80] Si Luna
in principio egritudinis est sine aspectu et in die termini[13] eam aspi-
ciat aliquis planetarum bonus vel malus, innovabitur super egrum
aliquod bonum vel malum secundum naturam planete, de quo non
cogitabatur. [81] Si Luna eclipsatur quando est in quarto loco principii egritudinis vel in opposito, est malum signum secundum modum eclipsis. [82] Si signum ascendens in principio egritudinis erit
caput Arietis vel Libre et Luna erit in una de cavillis, in tali casu termini erunt firmi absque dubio, et hoc quando Luna erit in quadrato
vel eius opposito. [83] Si Luna in principio egritudinis est in signo
mobili, significat properationem egri in bono vel malo. Et si est in
signo stabili, elongabitur egritudo. Si est in signo medio, mutabitur
egritudo ab una in aliam. [84] Si est causa egritudinis multiplicatio
humorum in corpore et lux Lune crescit, est valde durum. Et si lux
eius minuitur, est melius. [85] Et si causa egritudinis est diminutio et
lux Lune diminuitur, est durum. Et si crescit, est melius. [86] Si Luna
in principio egritudinis est in signo nature humoris qui generat egritudinem, est durum. [87] Et si est in signo contrario egritudini, est
bonum signum. Et totum hoc est verum si non habet coniunctionem
cum planeta vel aspectum ad illum, quia si haberet, iudicandum esset secundum aspectum vel coniunctionem.

[88] Coniunctio Lune cum Saturno significat malum et lon-
gitudinem egritudinis, et specialiter cum Lune lumen diminuitur.
[89] Attamen quando est in augmento luminis, modicum dampni-
ficat Saturnum. Et si Saturnus est tardus in suo cursu, multiplicatur
in malo. Et si est/f. 87v/velox, diminuitur. [90] Et si est retrogradus
et ante oppositum Solis, postquam sanatus erit reinfirmabitur egro-
tus. [91] Si Saturnus est in loco sue altitudinis vel prope eum et eger
est constipatus, multiplicabitur malum super malum. Et si est in
suo descensu, minuetur malum. Et si eger est laxus, et Saturnus est
in suo descensu, multiplicabitur malum super malo. Et si est in sua

altitudine, minuetur malum. [92] Si Luna est cum Iove vel in eius aspectu sexto vel tertio, est valde bonum signum, maxime illi qui transivit medietatem suorum dierum. Et etiam aspectus oppositus vel quadratus significat bonum, sed cum labore egri.

[93] Et hoc est quod deliberavi comprehendere in hoc tractatu, et est leve omni medico scienti scire, si de hiis servire sibi voluerit, et est iustius et verius secundum experimentatores. [94] Et si aliquando peccat, non est mirum, quia multotiens accidet vel per demonstrationes nativitatis egri que non sunt concordantes demonstrationibus habitis a temporibus egritudinis et boaran, et ille demonstrationes nativitatis sunt principales (?), vel per confessionem et bona opera que frangunt sententiam hominis vel per esse occultum omnes radices huius scientie a medico, quia impossibile est eas omnes in hoc tractatu comprehendere.

[95] Totum tamen est in potestate Dei, qui est medicus omnis carnis et est magnus et faciens mirabilia magna solus et nullus alius ab ipso, *qui vivit et regnat in secula seculorum, amen.*

Notes

1. Fols 16v–22v. For a full description of the contents of this manuscript see C. Burnett, 'The *kitāb al-Isṭamāṭīs* and a Manuscript of Astrological and Astronomical Works from Barcelona (Biblioteca de Catalunya, 634)', in idem, *Magic and Divination in the Middle Ages*, Aldershot, 1996, article VII.

2. These are the degrees within each sign over which each of the planets (not the Sun and the Moon) are said to rule in turn. In Table I the relative 'strengths' (*virtutes*) of being in a house or exaltation or being lord of a triplicity or a term are given.

3. The signs are similarly divided into 'ninth-parts' and 'twelfth-parts,' ruled in turn by the planets and the Sun and Moon.

4. For a convenient English version of Ibn Ezra's text see R. Levy, *The Beginning of Wisdom, An Astrological Treatise by Abraham ibn Ezra, an edition of the Old French Version of 1273 and an English Translation of the Hebrew Original*, Baltimore, 1939.

5. Pseudo-Ptolemy, *Centiloquium*, verbum 9.

6. I.e., the tables at the end of the text.

7. Scribe adds in margin: narratio vocabulorum.

8. See Table V.

9. Scribe writes in the margin: de impedimentis <Lune>.

10. Hebrew implies 'post' ('after').

11. *In the margin:* id est accessionum, quia septima accessio est cretica in febri tertiana et quartana, sed in febri continua dies septimus est creticus.

12. The scribe adds in the margin: nota has regulas.

13. In the margin: i.e. diei cretici.

Table I, f. 88r[1]

virtutes / *signa*	.5. *domus*	.4. *honor*	.3. *triplicitas in die et nocte*			2 *termini*
Aries: diurnus, ignis, masculinum, mobile, indirectum, orientale, calidum et siccum	Martis	Sol .19.	Sol .2.	Iupiter 1	Saturnus	Iupiter 6 Venus 6 Mercurius 8 Mars 5 Saturnus 5 / Tolomeus: (Venus)² 8 (Mercurius) 7 (Saturnus) 4
Taurus: nocturnus, terra, femininum, stabile, indirectum, frigidum et siccum, meridionale	Veneris	Luna .3.	Venus	Luna	Mars	Venus 8 Mercurius 5³ Iupiter 8 Saturnus 5 Mars 3 / Tolomeus: (Mercurius) 8 (Iupiter) 8 Mars 2 Saturnus 6
Geminis: diurnus, aer, masculinum, medium seu duo corpora, indirectum, occidentale, calidum et humidum	Mercurii	Caput draconis .3.	Saturnus	Mercurius	Iupiter	Mercurius 6 Iupiter 6 Venus 5 Mars 7 Saturnus 6 / Tolomeus: (Mercurius) 7 (Venus) 7 (Mars) 6 (Saturnus) 4
Cancer: nocturnus, aqua, femininum, mobile, directum, frigidum et humidum, septentrionale, estivale	Lune	Iupiter .15.	Venus	Mars	Luna	Mars 7 Venus 6 Mercurius 6 Iupiter 7 Saturnus 4 / Tolomeus: Mars 6 Iupiter 6 Mercurius 7 Venus 7 Saturnus 4

Leo: diurnus, igneus, masculinum, stabile, calidum et siccum, orientale, directum, estivale	Solis	Altitudo Martis in xii°	Sol	Iupiter	Saturnus	Iupiter 6 Venus 5 Saturnus 7 Mars 6 Mercurius 6[4] Tolomeus: Saturnus 6 Mercurius 7 Venus 6, Mars 6, Iupiter 5
Virgo: nocturnum, terreum, femininum, duo corpora, directum, frigidum et siccum temperatum, meridionale, estivale	Mercurii	Mercurii .15.	Venus	Luna	Mars	Mercurius 7 Venus 10 Iupiter 4 Mars 7 Saturnus 2 Tolomeus: (Mercurius) 7 (Venus) 6 (Iupiter) 10 (Mars) 5 (Saturnus) 2
Libra: diurnus, aeris, masculinum, mobile, directum, calidum et humidum, occidentale, autumpnale	Veneris	Saturnus .21.	Saturnus	Mercurius	Iupiter	Saturnus 6 Mercurius 8 Iupiter 7 Venus 7 Mars 2 Tolomeus: Saturnus 6 Venus 5 Iupiter 8 Mercurius 5 Mars 6
Scorpius: nocturnum aqua, femininum, stabile, directum, frigidum et humidum, septentrionale, autumpnale	Martis	.0.	Venus	Mars	Luna	Mars 7 Venus 4 Mercurius 8 Iupiter 5 Saturnus 6 Tolomeus: Mars 6 Mercurius 6 Iupiter 7 Venus 6 Saturnus 5
Sagittarius: diurnum, ignis, masculinum, orientale, temperatum, directum, autumpnale, duo corpora	Iovis	honor Caude draconis .3.	Sol	Iupiter	Saturnus	Iupiter 12 Venus 5 Mercurius 4 Saturnus 5 Mars 4 Tolomeus: (Iupiter) 8 (Venus) 6 (Mercurius) 5 (Saturnus) 6 (Mars) 5

(continues)

Table I, f. 88r[1] Continued.

virtutes signa	.5. domus	.4. honor	.3. triplicitas in die et nocte			2. termini
Capricornus: nocturnum, terra, femininum, directum, mobile, meridionale, frigidum et siccum.	Saturni	Mars .28.	Venus	Luna	Mars	Mercurius 7 Iupiter 7 Venus 8 Saturnus 4 Mars 5 / Tolomeus: Venus 6 Mercurius 6 Iupiter 7 Saturnus 6 Mars 5
Aquarius: diurnum, aer, masculinus, stabile, directum, occidentale	Saturni	.0.	Saturnus	Mercurius	Iupiter	Mercurius 7 Venus 6 Iupiter 7 Mars 5 Saturnus 5 / Tolomeus: Saturnus 6 Mercurius 6 Iupiter 5 Mars 5 Venus 8
Piscis: nocturnum, aque, femininum, indirectum, duo corpora, temperatum, septentrionale	Iovis	Venus .27.	Venus	Mars	Luna	Venus 12 Iupiter 4 Mercurius 3 Mars 9 Saturnus 2 / Tolomeus: (Venus) 8 (Iupiter) 6 (Mercurius) 6 (Mars) 5 (Saturnus) 5

Termini veri termini Egyptorum non termini Tolomei

[1]Not all differences from Abraham Ibn Ezra's *Beginning of Wisdom* have been noted here. Some could be due to transcription errors in these tables.

[2]In the table the variant values of Ptolemy are often simply placed under the values of the Egyptians (the first row); in these cases the relevant planets have been put in brackets.

[3]This should be '6.'

[4]This should be 'Mercurius 6, Mars 6'.

Table II, f. 88v

signa	*facies*	*vile*	*malivolencia*	*novene*
Aries	Mars, Sol, Iupiter Indiani: (3)[5] Venus	Saturnus .21.	Venus .25.	Mars 1, 8, Venus 2, 7, Mercurius 3, 6, Luna 4, Sol 5, Iupiter 9
Taurus	Venus,[6] Luna, Saturnus Indiani: (2) Mercurius	Mars	Caput draconis Martis et domus sue letiticie	Saturnus 1, 2, Iupiter 3, Mars 4, Venus 5, Mercurius 6, 9, Luna 7, Sol 8
Geminis	Iupiter, Mars, Sol Indiani: Mercurius, Venus, Saturnus	Saturnus, bisextus eius in .xii.°	Iupiter et locus altitudinis Solis	Venus 1, 8, Mars 2, 7, Iupiter 3, 6, Saturnus 4, 5, Mercurius 9
Cancer	Venus, Mercurius, Luna Indiani: Luna, Mars, Iupiter	Mars .28.	Infernus draco Iovis in .9. gradu et draco Saturni in .19.	Luna 1, Sol 2, Mercurius 3, Venus 4, Mars 5, Iupiter 6, 9, Saturnus 7, 8
Leo	Saturnus, Iupiter, Mars Indiani: (1) Sol	Saturnus	altitudo Martis in .25.°	Mars 1, 8, Venus 2, 7, Mercurius 3, 6, Luna 4, Sol 5, Iupiter 9
Virgo	Sol, Venus, Mercurius Indiani: Mercurius, Saturnus, Venus	Venus .27.	Iupiter	Saturnus 1, 2, Iupiter 3, Mars 4, Venus 5, Mercurius 6, 9, Luna 7, Sol 8
Libra	Luna, Saturnus, Iupiter Indiani: Venus, Saturnus, Mercurius	Sol .19.	Mars, altitudo Mercurii in .25. gradibus	Venus 1, 8, Mars 2, 7, Iupiter 3, 6, Saturnus 4, 5, Mercurius 9
Scorpius	Mars, Sol, Venus Indiani: (2) Iupiter, (3) Luna	Luna .3.	Venus	Luna 1, Sol 2, Mercurius 3, Venus 4, Mars 5, Iupiter 6, 9, Saturnus 7, 8
Sagittarius	Mercurius, Luna, Saturnus Indiani: Iupiter, Mars, Sol		Mercurius, altitudo Saturni in .xii.°	Mars 1, 8, Venus 2, 7, Merucrius 3, 6, Luna 4, Sol 5, Iupiter 9
Capri-cornus	Iupiter, Mars, Sol Indiani: (1) Saturnus (2), Venus	Iupiter .25.[7]	Luna	Saturnus 1, 2, Iupiter 3, Mars 4, Venus 5, Mercurius 6, 9, Luna 7, Sol 8
Aquarius	Venus, Mercurius, Luna Indiani: Saturnus, Mercurius, Venus		Sol et bisextus Martis in .xii.°	Venus 1, 8, Mars 2, 7, Iupiter 3, 6, Saturnus 4, 5, Mercurius 9
Piscis	Saturnus, Iupiter, Luna, Mars Indiani: Iupiter, Luna, Mars	Mercurius .15.	malivolentia Lune in .xv.° et bisextus Iovis in .xxiii.°	Luna 1, Sol 2, Mercurius 3, Venus 4, Mars 5, Iupiter 6, 9, Saturnus 7, 8

Facies vere facies Indorum

[5]The numbers in brackets indicate whether the Indians make the planet lord of the first, second, or third decan.

[6]This should be 'Mercurius.'

[7]This should be '15'.

Table III, f. 89r

signa	virtus .xii.
Aries	Mars 1, 8, Venus 2, 7, Mercurius 3, 6, Luna 4, Sol 5, Iupiter 9, 12, Saturnus 10, 11
Taurus	Venus 1, 6, Mercurius 2, 5, Luna 3, Sol 4, Mars 7, 12, Iupiter 8, 11, Saturnus 9, 10
Geminis	Mercurius 1, 4, Luna 2, Sol 3, Venus 5, 12, Mars 6, 11, Iupiter 7, 10, Saturnus 8, 9
Cancer	Luna 1, Sol 2, Mercurius 3, 12, Venus 3, 10, Mars 4, 9, Iupiter 5, 8, Saturnus 6, 7, Luna 12[8]
Leo	Sol 1, Mercurius 2, 11, Venus 3, 10, Mars 4, 9, Iupiter 5, 8, Saturnus 6, 7, Luna 12
Virgo	Mercurius 1, 10, Venus 2, 9, Mars 3, 8, Iupiter 4, 7, Saturnus 5, 6, Luna 11, Sol 12
Libra	Venus 1, 8, Mars 2, 7, Iupiter 3, 6, Saturnus 4, 5, Mercurius 9, 12, Luna 10, Sol 11
Scorpius	Mars 1, 6, Iupiter 2, 5, Saturnus 3, 4, Venus 7, 12, Mercurius 8, 11, Luna 9, Sol 10
Sagittarius	Iupiter 1, 4, Saturnus 2, 3, Mars 5, 12, Venus 6, 11, Mercurius 7, 10, Luna 8, Sol 9
Capricornus	Saturnus 1, 2, Iupiter 3, 12, Mars 4, 11, Venus 5, 10, Mercurius 6, 9, Luna 7, Sol 8
Aquarius	Saturnus 1, 12, Iupiter 2, 11, Mars 3, 10, Venus 4, 9, Mercurius 5, 8, Luna 5[9], Sol 7
Piscis	Iupiter 1, 10, Mars 2, 9, Venus 3, 8, Mercurius 4, 7, Luna 5, Sol 6, Saturnus 11, 12

[8]This should be 'Luna 1, Sol 2, Mercurius 3, 12, Venus 4, 11, Mars 5, 10, Iupiter 6, 9, Saturn 7, 8.'
[9]This should be '6.'

Table IV, f. 89v

condiciones	*signa*	*membra*	*egritudines*
hore eius addite, ascensiones diminute, forma quatuor pedum, vox media	Aries	caput, facies, pupilla oculi, aures	epilencia, dolor aurium, naris, decite (?), oculorum, macularum
hore eius addite, ascensiones diminute, quatuor pedum, vox media	Taurus	collum, gutur	porcellane sive truges, tortura colli seu glandule, gibositas
hore eius addite, ascensiones diminute, forma hominis	Geminis	spatule, brachia, armus, manus	omnis infirmitas sanguinis, et omnis morbus qui accidit in membris predictis
hore eius longe, ascensiones addite, forma uteris aque	Cancer	pectus, mamille, coste, latera, splen, pulmo, iecur	omne quod accidit in dictis membris et gravitas oculorum
hore eius longe, ascensiones longe, forma quatuor pedum, vox media	Leo	pectus, cor, stomacus, viscera superiora, vene dorsum, lumbi, coste, nuclea	morbus membrorum predictorum
hore longe, ascensiones longe, forma hominis et forma avis, vox fortis	Virgo	venter, intestina, diafragma, iliace	infirmitas membrorum predictorum et omnis morbus proveniens ex malencolia
hore breves, ascensiones longe, forma hominis	Libra	quod est subtus ventrem prope membrum virile, vel sexum muliebre et clunes et renes	retentio urine et sanguis inferius descendens et obscuritas oculorum
hore breves, ascensiones longe, forma scorpionis	Scorpius	verecundus locus id est pecten, membrum viri et sexus mulieris seu virga virilis, vulva et anus	macula oculorum, cancer, verola, lepra, macule sive pigues faciei, calvities, <i>moroyde
hore breves,	Sagittarius	genitivos et	

Table IV, f. 89v

condiciones	signa	membra	egritudines
hore breves, ascensiones longe, forma media hominis et media equi	Sagittarius	genitivos et membrum additum seu superfluum et crura seu femora	cecitas, calvicies, cadere de alto, morbus proveniens ex veneno et morsibus silvestrium et propter incisionem membri
hore breves, ascensiones breves	Capricornus	genua	genua, verola, lepra, mutuitas, surditas, calvicies, obfuscatio occulorum et sanguis qui descendit ad inferiora
hore breves, ascensiones breves, forma hominis	Aquarius	tibie et earum caville	infirmitas tibiarum, malencolia, ictericia nigra, incisio venarum, vacce (?)
hore breves, ascensiones breves	Piscis	pedes et digiti eorum	infirmitas pedum et digitorum eorum, gracella, lepra et generaliter est signum infirmitatum

Table V, f. 90r

planete et eorum complectiones	membra corporis	egritudines	virtus corporis planetarum
Saturnus: frigidus et siccus, malus, dampnosus, masculinus, diurnus	ossa, melsa, auris dexter (*sic*), vesica, colera	vesania, tremor, paralisis, apoplexia, lepra, infirmitas pedum	.9.
Iupiter: calidus et humidus, bonus, masculinus, diurnus	auris sinistra, dura, coste et omnis sanguis	infirmitas levis, cito transiens	.9.
Mars: calidus, siccus, ardens, dampnosus, femininus, nocturnus	fel, nar dester, sanguis venarum, renes, virga virilis, torela (?), sanguis adustus	febris unica, etica, bamboles rubee, timor, vesania, ulcera	.8.
Sol: calidus et siccus, prodest et nocet, masculinus, diurnus	cor, oculus dexter in die et nocte, cerebrum, vene, medietas dextra totius corporis	omne accidens oris	.15.
Venus: frigidus et humidus, bonus, femininus, nocturnus	caro, sagimen, pinguedo, epar, sperma, omnes humores	omne quod accidit renibus et in locis turpibus et occultis, ut in pectine.	.7.
Mercurius: temperatus, mobilis, declinans ad frigiditatem et siccitatem	Lingua, ors (*sic*), arterie, et habet partem in sanguine	infirmitas anime, ut ymaginatio, tristicia et iracundia	.7.
Luna: frigida et humida, cum modico calore, feminina nocturnus (*sic*)	In die oculus sinister et in nocte pulmo et gutur, viscera superiora, matrix, totum latus sinistrum	communis infirmitas ex habundantia humoris	.12.

Dicit Aristoteles in libro de secre<tis> c<apitulo> de proprietate lapidum quod gradus et dispositio planetarum et lapidum mineralium secundum essentiam recipit for[mam] vincentem et dominantem in eo secundum originem et naturam a superioribus naturis, unde vincens in plantis est natura aque et in mineralibus [et lapi]dibus vincens est natura terrea. Recipit ergo natura plantarum extensionem de natura aquarum sicut aqua recipit extensionem per [impe]tum et impulsionem ventorum in suo loco, et sicut aqua est diversarum figurarum, quia in aqua sunt multe figure, sic accidit in plantis [quod] omnes figure inveniuntur in plantis. Cum itaque vincens in plantis sit aqua et non extenditur nisi per diffusionem, et operator d[iso]lutionis vel diffusionis aquarum sit perpetuus et incessanter operans in suo celo, scilicet Mercurius, quomodo universaliter verum est quod unusquisque [pla]neta regit et disponit quod convenit et assimilatur sue nature. Verbi gratia, Saturnus tenet terram, Mercurius aquam, Iupiter aerem, [Mars] ignem, et non reperitur hec convenientia in operibus planetarum vel eorum corporibus sed in oppositionibus vel operationibus quod semper habent continuas virtutes perpetuas per superiorem virtutem universalem que est super omnes virtutes istarum operationum etc.

Chapter Four

Modern English Translation

*S*ays David Ben Rabbi Yom Tov:

[1] Since—as has already been explained[1] the forms in[2] the world of composite things are subordinate[3] to the forms of the spheres and receive from them every kind of impression and change; and since astrology,[4] i.e. its theoretical[5] part, studies the ways in which change effected by the force of the spheres occurs in the world of the elements; while <also> the movement from health to illness and vice versa is a change; and since medicine studies this change[6] in <human> bodies; there is necessarily some relationship and overlap (or: common ground; *shittuf*) between these two arts, i.e. medicine and that part of astrology which we mentioned above.

[2] Knowledge of the art of medicine, of the <different> natures of individuals[7] and of <other> medical things is part of the perfection of the astrologer so that he can avail himself of the force[8] of the spheres and prepare those who are passive to receive the effect of the agents [or: active forces] or that he can repel much[9] of the effect of the agents if he wants to. [3] Similarly, knowledge of the forces of the spheres and their application on individuals is part of the perfection of the physician. Thus he[10] will understand the effects of the distant and proximate agents on passive things [i.e. he will understand from the aspect of the action of cause]) and also that passive things are disposed towards this [i.e. he will understand from the aspect of the disposition of passive bodies to receive these forces]. Therefore, he[11] will be able to make a prognosis about good and bad crises, better than he had been able to do on the basis of his art alone. Neither a scholar nor a common man will raise doubts about this.

[4] However, since—as Hippocrates said[12]—<human> life is too short[13] and every one of these arts is too long, so that one cannot reach perfection and completeness in even one of them, but only [some of] its many parts,[14] no one lives long enough to master all of the subdisciplines <of medicine and astrology>, let alone that one would live long enough to master both arts completely. [5] For the hearts have grown smaller and[15] those of the latter generations are like a very fine needle. It[16] is therefore impossible that anyone can be found to master both arts, and if such a person would be found, it would be an uncommonly wondrous thing.

[6] It is better for every human being to master one science than to know a little bit of this and a little bit of that. Therefore, only rarely can one find a physician with knowledge of astrology although it is necessary for his art as[17] we have said. [7] Sometimes[18] they go to those who do have this knowledge or to those of whom they think that they have this knowledge and accordingly choose the times for their treatment.[19]

[8] Therefore, a distinguished friend and[20] one of the experts in medicine in our time has asked me—since he thought something that is not so[21] —to[22] compose a concise summary (*kelal qaṭan*) of astrology which a physician needs every day for the administration of purgatives, potions and vomitives, and bleedings, for these things are always <needed> and their execution needs careful consideration in order to be successful. [9] I[23] knew that, were I to say "I do not know" <enough astrology to write the book>, I would not <be able to> maintain that which I do know, since it would become publicized that I do not know. And since I know my own worth, I refused to turn him down so that he would not think that I would refuse to satisfy him.[24] [10] I therefore granted his request according to my ability[25] from the books composed on this subject. I did not contribute anything new of my own. Now I will begin, may God[26] help me.

[11] I say that anyone who wants to use this concise summary (*kelal qaṭan*),[27] should first of all learn to compute the daily positions of the seven planets from the almanac. [12] To learn this is very easy even for someone who knows no theory at all.[28] [13] This holds especially true for the five planets, namely, Saturn, Jupiter, Mars, Sun, and Mercury, for their positions can be learned in a very easy and quick way.[29] [14] But the computation of Venus and the Moon is difficult and somewhat complicated for someone who is not used to it. Therefore, if someone wants to make an exact and correct computation of them he needs some practice in its study. [15] Al-

ternatively, he can have the positions of those planets (Venus and the Moon) computed over many days and years—something that could also be obtained from experts.[30] [16] Equally, he should have with him the astronomical tables which are usually written at the end of the almanac. These tables, which are excerpted in a concise way by the astrologers from the books on this science and which provide easy and quick information about the natures of the signs, the planets, their houses, their apogee and perigee, their exaltation, detriment and fall, their triplicity, limit and decan [17] and about the other things necessary for this treatise—I thought it good to select from these tables that which is vital for the intention of this treatise, for not every one has astronomical tables. [18] Only a few things amongst those which I selected are not vital for this treatise. I appended them (the astrological tables) so that if someone has this treatise he does not have to search after those tables. Instead, along with this treatise, he needs only to know the positions of the planets in one of the ways[31] I mentioned. [19] Once he is able to learn the positions of the planets in one of the ways mentioned[32] and the other things which he should know according to the intention of this treatise, he can use <this information> on his own for the selection of the times proper for purgatives, bleedings and vomitives.[33] He does not have to ask an astrologer or experienced astronomer.[34]

[20] Now that we have set forth what someone who wants to use this treatise should know I will begin according to my intention and will first of all give an explanation of the terms used by the masters of this science which feature in this treatise.[35] [21] It is said that one planet is in conjunction with another planet when it is in the same sign <as the other>, and each of the planets is within the strength of the body[36] of the other. The strength of the body of each of the planets can be found in the tables attached to the almanac[37] mentioned before. [22] Quartile aspect occurs when the <elongation> between two planets is 90°, opposition <when it is> 180°, trine <when it is> 120°, and sextile <when it is> 60°. [23] All these aspects have the strength of the aspect even if the aspect falls short by <a quantity> less than 6°,[38] whether above or below the degree of the aspect. [24] For instance, if <the elongation> between two stars is 96° or 84°,[39] the aspect is quartile; but the[40] harm caused by each planet is not as strong as when the aspect is exact. So also for the other aspects. [25] It is said of a planet that it exerts its might when it is in its own house or in[41] the house of its exaltation or in[42] the house of its triplicity or in its limit or decan,[43] and forms a

conjunction or aspect with another planet. <As to> the houses, exaltation, triplicity, limit and decan, all this can be determined from the tables attached[44] to the almanac.

[26] The Ascendant is the sign rising in the east each hour. It can be known[45] by means of instruments[46] or tables; or approximately through the hours of the day by adding one sign to the degree of the Sun for every two hours that have passed since it rose. This last method is a very approximate one; the only way to determine it <exactly> is through tables or instruments. [27] The Lord of the rising sign is called "The Lord of the Ascendant."[47] A planet which[48] is called "retrograde" can be known from the[49] almanac. In the same way one can know a planet rising in the orb of its apogee or <a planet> descending in it. The degree of apogee can be known from the above-mentioned tables attached[50] to the almanac.[51] [28] When it is before the degree of apogee, less than 90°, it is called "rising," and when it is after the degree of apogee, less than 90°, it is called "descending." The degree of perigee lies opposite the degree of apogee.

[29] Good or benefic planets are Jupiter, Venus, the Sun and the Moon when the Moon is not suffering from one of the corruptions described below. Similarly, although Jupiter, Venus and the Sun are mostly benefics, it is possible that their power and beneficial[52] influence are[53] weakened. Saturn and Mars are malefic, and Mercury is generally so <i.e. malefic>. [30] That which is opposite the ascending sign is called "the seventh house."[54] It is said of a planet that it is in the house of its detriment when it is in the sign opposite to <that of> its house. [31] Tropical signs[55] are Aries, Libra, Cancer and Capricorn. Fixed signs are Taurus, Leo, Scorpio and Aquarius. Bicorporal signs are Gemini, Virgo, Sagittarius and Pisces.

[32] It is said of planet that it is slow[56] in motion when its motion in one day is less than its mean motion. The mean <daily> motion of Saturn is 0;2,1. It is fast when its motion in one day is more than its mean motion. The mean <daily> motion of the Moon is 13;10°. [33] Corruption of the Moon <can occur> in many ways: One of them is that it is eclipsed. The second is that it is closer than twelve degrees to the Sun, going towards it or separating from it. The third is that between it and the degree of its opposition are less than 12 degrees before or after it. The fourth is that it is in conjunction or aspect with malefics. The fifth is that it is in Saturn's or Mars's dodecatemorion. This can be derived from the above-mentioned tables. The sixth is that it is with the Head or Tail of the nodes or that there is less than 12 degrees between them. The seventh is

that it is in the end of the sign. The eighth is that it is between 19°
Libra and 3° Scorpio. The ninth is that it is slow in its motion.[57] So
much for the explanation of the terms featuring in this treatise.

[34] I will <now> start to mention the rules necessary according to the intention of this treatise.[58] If you want to perform
bloodletting, be careful not to do so when the Moon is in the sign
of Gemini or when it is <in conjunction> with Saturn or Mars[59] or
when it forms the aspect of a quartile or opposition with them or
with Mercury.[60] But an aspect of a trine or sextile is better than one
of these aspects with Saturn. [35] In general, be careful not to use
an iron <instrument> for surgery in[61] one of the parts of the body
when the Moon is in the sign indicating[62] that part <of the body>.[63]
[36] For instance, if you want to perform surgery in the head or[64] to
let blood from it, do not do so as long as the Moon is in Aries which
is the sign of the head. If you want to let blood from the neck, <do
not do so> as long as the Moon is in Taurus, the sign of the neck.[65]
And so also with regard to all of the other <parts of the body>. This
has been tested by experience,[66] and[67] it is accepted by the consensus of both the ancient and modern <authorities.>[68]

[37] If you want to administer a foodstuff or potion in order
to purge <the body of a patient>, do so when the Moon is in a sign
similar to the humor which you want to expel.[69] [38] For instance, if
you want to expel yellow bile, do so when the Moon is in <one of>
the fiery signs,[70] namely, Aries, Leo and Sagittarius. And[71] black
bile, when the Moon is in <one of> the earthy signs except for Capricorn, namely, Taurus and Virgo. If you want to expel phlegm, do
so when the Moon is in <one of> the watery signs, namely, Cancer,
Scorpio and Pisces. And if you want to expel blood, i.e., to perform
bloodletting,[72] do so when the Moon is in one of the airy signs,
namely, Gemini, Libra and Aquarius. [39] But you should observe
the condition mentioned above, namely, that the Moon is not in
the sign of the bodily part that you want to bleed. [40] If you want
to expel bodily fluids in general, i.e.,[73] more than one fluid, you
should do so when the Moon is in one of the watery signs. [41] If
you do so when the Moon is in the sign of Scorpio, take care that
she has passed 3° Scorpio, and if you can take care that no other
planet will aspect her, that would be even better.

[42] Whatever purgative you intend to give, take care that
<when you administer it> the Moon does not give her power to one
of the <other> planets above the horizon,[74] and that the Lord of the
Ascendant is not in conjunction with a planet above the horizon, for
if that is the case he will regurgitate the potion.[75] [43] And if <at that

moment> the Moon gives her power to <one of the> planets under the horizon it is not harmful, but only if it does not give her power in a bad aspect to one of the malefics or to a retrograde planet, for this also indicates that he will regurgitate the potion. [44] If at the moment that you administer a purgative Saturn aspects the Moon while it rises in the orbit of its apogee, it indicates that the purgative will not purge in a proper way. But if it is descending in the orbit of its apogee, it[76] indicates that it will purge more than necessary. [45] According to Ptolemy, one should also take care when one administers a purgative that the Moon is not <in aspect> with Jupiter or Venus or gives its power to them, for then the effect of the purgative would diminish and weaken.[77] [46] However, later astrologers did not agree with him, as is attested by the learned R. Abraham <Ibn Ezra>. For according to his opinion one should—when possible—take care that the Moon does not aspect Mercury.[78]

[47] If you want to administer an emetic, you should do so when the Moon is in the sign of Taurus or when it gives its power to a planet that is in[79] Taurus or to a planet which is above the horizon or retrograde. [48] If you want to bathe a patient—whatever[80] patient it may be—you should do so when the Moon is in one of the watery signs or in any sign on condition that it aspects[81] one of the benefics or that it forms any aspect with the Sun except for opposition. [49] So much for what can be found in the books which we have on this science about the selection of the <proper> times to administer potions[82] and purgatives and to perform bleedings. [50] According to the principles and fundamentals of this science it is possible to find other elections[83] and proper and improper times besides those which we mentioned. However, it is impossible to give a general rule regarding this matter. Only by means of knowledge of the principles and[84] methods of this science <can those times be determined>.[85] Yet what we have written about it might[86] be enough for our purpose.

[51] I thought that it would be a good thing to add to this some short sayings and rules which it would be good[87] for a physician to know and which will be of assistance to him, in addition to his knowledge of medicine. Some of them deal with the treatment given by the physician to the patient and others deal with a prognosis of what will happen to the patient. For[88] the physician should know all of these things which belong to his science as well as possible.

[52] Ptolemy said: When the seventh <house> and its Lord are harmed in[89] a patient, give the patient[90] another physician.[91] He means by this that the Ascendant and its Lord indicate the patient

while the seventh <house> and its Lord indicate the physician. Therefore, when the seventh house and its Lord are harmed because of a malefic conjunction or aspect, it points to an error or mistake by the physician, who should for this reason be replaced.[92] [53] Although this statement is directed against the physician he should nevertheless be familiar with it, for nobody is free from mistakes— and "who can understand mistakes?"[93] A good physician, one who aims to bring health to the patient, should[94] not be so faulty as to refrain from this <i.e. taking himself off the case> for the sake of his honor. [54] When he sees these signs he should suspect that he made a mistake in recognizing the cause[95] of the disease or that the <correct> ways to treat it were hidden from him. Therefore, he should request to be replaced or to engage another physician next to himself and thus do what is correct and good[96] and get a good name.[97]

[55] I do not know what cause the learned physicians adduce for the days in which the crisis falls, nor whether their opinion about it is based on experience only or on logical reasoning. But I have seen expert physicians become alarmed[98] when they saw a good and complete crisis on a day on which a crisis does not fall according to the medical science and could not give a reason for it. [56] But men of this science[99] adduce a cause for these things and say that the cause for these crises is that[100] the Moon is in well-known configurations[101] with respect to its position in the beginning of a disease. [57] They compare this to the action of a wise litigant towards a foolish one.[102] For the disease overwhelms Nature at the beginning, but she [Nature] makes no move to defeat it at that time. <Instead,> she waits until the Moon arrives at a position contrary to that in which it was at the beginning of the disease so that the power of the matter moved by it <the disease> will not be as it was at the beginning of the disease. And then <Nature> awakens to overcome its opponent. [58] For when the Moon is in a position opposite to it,[103] crises[104] occur and will be right, proper and beneficial or bad according to the configuration of the Moon with respect to its position at the beginning of the disease. [59] And according to the aspects of the planets with her—the strongest of which is opposition—the most true and right crisis for good or for bad will be <on> the fourteenth day.[105] Then the Moon has arrived opposite its <initial> position. [60] For instance, if we find the Moon at the beginning of the disease in the beginning of Aries, it will arrive at the opposite of this position on the fourteenth day of the disease. [61] The opposite of this position is Libra which is the opposite of Aries in the quality

affected by it. Similarly, all oppositions are necessarily contrary to one another either in the quality active <in them> or in the quality affected <by them> or in both and this (i.e. that they are contrary to both) is <true> for most <cases>. [62] Similarly, when it attains quartile <aspect> with its position <at the onset of illness>, namely, on the seventh day, it also arrives at a position which is contrary to its position at the beginning of the disease in one of the abovementioned qualities. [63] It is therefore said that the crisis occurs on the seventh day when the Moon forms the aspect of a quartile with its position at the beginning of the disease. And on the fourteenth day <when it forms> the aspect of opposition and on the twentieth or twenty-first day <when it forms> the aspect of a second quartile, while on the twenty-seventh or twenty-eighth day it returns to its position at the beginning of the disease.[106] [64] And although there is no contrariness in qualities in that position,[107] sometimes there is a good crisis.[108] For after all the aspects have passed and contrary qualities have been activated, and a strengthening of the disease has been prevented, the power of the matter[109] is so much weakened that the disease is declining. [65] And when the Moon returns to its position at the beginning of the disease, Nature moves to overcome the disease in a reinvigorated fashion.[110] [66] A reason is also given[111] for the other days of crises. It is said: The fifth day is a day of a crisis because it (i.e. the Moon) forms the aspect of a sextile with its initial position where it was at the beginning of the disease. Similarly, on the eleventh day it will form the aspect of a trine with its position at the beginning of the disease. The seventeenth day is like the eleventh day and the twenty-fourth like the fifth day.[112]

[67] The reason that crises fall on the other days is that the Moon is sometimes fast in its motion so that it arrives on the fourth or sixth <day> at a position which it only reaches[113] on the fifth or seventh day when it is slow in its motion. This is why a crisis appears earlier, namely, on the fourth or on the sixth day and similarly at the end of the ninth <day> instead of the eleventh.[114] [68] Sometimes it is slow in its motion and arrives at the beginning of the ninth <day> at a position at which it arrives at other times on the seventh <day>. [69] For this reason the crisis sometimes falls on the fourth, sixth and ninth <day>, and for this very same reason it is sometimes seen on other days on which a crisis <normally> does not fall but which are adjacent to a day of crisis, namely, on the tenth, thirteenth, nineteenth, twentieth and twenty-eighth <day>. [70] As for the days after[115] the twenty-eighth, the physicians already said that the crisis will fall on them every seven days. The reason for

this is that, because of the fact that the disease has become chronic, Nature has not overcome it when the Moon returns to the position in which it was at the beginning of the disease. [71] It can therefore only become active when the Moon returns to the aspect of a quartile or opposition with its <initial> position because these are strong aspects. [72] In general, when the Moon forms any aspect with its position at the beginning of a disease Nature awakens to overcome the disease. Nature wins or is defeated depending on whether it is aspected by benefics or malefics and their position in the sphere. [73] After the fortieth day no crisis can be distinguished on a certain day from the point of view of medicine because it cannot be determined by medicine.[116] [74] But an expert in this science <can distinguish it>[117] by means of the Sun. For the way of the Moon in acute diseases is <similar> to the way of the Sun in chronic diseases, but with different stipulations.[118] However, to relate these would be too lengthy in this treatise. [75] In the case of intermittent fevers the ratio of the number of the cycles(?) is similar to the number of the days in continuous fevers.[119]

[76] An indication for a prognosis about the completeness of a crisis, its verification and its goodness or badness can be derived from the aspects of malefics or benefics with the above-mentioned positions of the Moon. For the benefics indicate goodness and that Nature will overcome the disease while the malefics indicate badness[120] unless it (i.e., the malefic) is opposite to the disease and the Moon within its limit. For then the aspect of the malefic will do no harm. [77] And although a discussion of this according to what is necessary would be lengthy and difficult for someone[121] who does not practice this art, I will nevertheless mention some general rules regarding this which are easy to know. [78] I say that if the Moon forms a quartile <aspect> with its position at the beginning of the disease or is in the aspect of opposition to it while it is in its own house or in the house of its exaltation, it is a semi good sign, although it neither forms a conjunction with Mercury nor forms an aspect with it. [79] The same holds good for the Sun if the disease persists. The opposite <is true> when they are in the house of their detriment or fall. [80] When the Moon is at the beginning of the disease without aspect <i.e. not aspected by any planet> but is on the[122] day of the limit aspected by a good or bad planet, something that has not been expected will occur to the patient and that is good or bad according to the nature of the planet.[123] [81] When the Moon is eclipsed while it forms <the aspect of> a quartile or opposition with its position at the beginning of the disease, it is a bad sign, according to the eclipse.[123]

[82] When at the beginning of the disease the rising sign is the beginning of Aries or Libra while the Moon is in one of the cardines, the crises will be certain without any doubt when the Moon arrives at quartile or opposition. [83] When the Moon at the beginning of the disease is in a tropical sign, it indicates that the[124] condition of the patient will change quickly for the good or the bad. When it is in a fixed sign the disease will be prolonged and when it is in a bicorporal sign he will suffer from one disease after another. [84] If the cause of the disease is an increase <of humors>[125] in the body while <also> the Moon is waxing, it is hard <to cure>. But when it is waning, it is better <for the cure of this type of illness>. [85] If the cause of the disease is a decrease <of humors in the body> while the Moon wanes it is grave.[126] But when it is waxing, it <i.e. the astrological indication> is better. [86] When the Moon is at the beginning of the disease in a sign corresponding to the nature of the humor which caused the disease, it is hard <to cure>. [87] But if it is in a sign opposite to the disease, it is a good indication; however, all this only holds good when the Moon does not form a conjunction with a planet and does not form an aspect with it. If this is the case, the judgment <of the outcome of the disease> is according to the aspect or conjunction.

[88] A conjunction of the Moon with Saturn indicates that the disease will be bad and prolonged, especially when it <i.e. the Moon> is waning. [89] But when the Moon waxes, the harm caused by Saturn will only be small, but when it (Saturn) is slow in its motion the harm will be worse and when it is fast it will not be that bad. [90] When it <Saturn> is retrograde and directly opposite[127] the Sun after the patient has been cured, he will fall ill <again>.[128] [91] When Saturn is in the position of its apogee or close to it while the[129] disease involves constipation, it will add evil to evil. And when it is in its perigee, the evil will be less. But when[130] the disease involves loose bowels and Saturn is in its perigee, it will <also> add evil to evil. And when it is in its apogee the evil will be less.[131] [92] When the Moon is <in conjunction> with Jupiter or forms the aspect of a sextile or trine with it, it is a very good indication, even more so for someone who is middle aged. Similarly, the aspect of opposition or quartile indicates something good, although it will only come slowly <or: with difficulty>.[132]

[93] This is what I wanted to include in this treatise which can be easily grasped by every learned physician and[133] man of understanding if he wants to use it. It is correct in most cases, as have testified experienced scholars.[134] [94] And if it fails sometimes, one should not be amazed about it, for this happens often

either because the indications of the natal horoscope of the patient do not correspond to the indications obtained from the times of the disease and the crisis[135]—and the indications <obtained> from the natal horoscope are the most significant. Moreover, it (i.e. the failure of the astrological prediction) may be due to repentance and good deeds which annul a <divine> decree, or because the physician does not know all the principles of this science which cannot be summarized and included in this treatise.[136] [95] But everything depends on God, blessed be He, the healer of all flesh who does wondrous deeds. There is no on else beside Him.[137]

Notes

1. L adds: "by Ptolemy in the Centiloquium" (i.e. verbum 9).

2. "in the world of composite things": "in this world" L.

3. "subordinate": "similar" L.

4. It is often quite difficult to draw a precise distinction between medieval astronomy and astrology. The *scientia stellarum* or *scientia astrorum* (*ḥokhmat ha-kokhavim*) encompassed both the *scientia motus*, the study of the movements of the spheres and planets (what we would call now "astronomy") and the *scientia iudicio-rum*, the study of the influence of those movements on man and world. See E.-Hui-zenga, "Die conste vanden almenack", *Queeste* 1 (1994): 12–33, p. 13, n. 5. S.-Pines, "The Semantic Distinction between the terms *Astronomy* and *Astrology* according to Al-Biruni," *Isis* 53 (1964), 343–349; repr., *The Collected Works of Shlomo Pines*, vol. 2 (Jerusalem and Leiden, 1986); French, R., *Astrology in medical practice, Practical Medicine from Salerno to the Black Death*, ed. L. García-Ballester, R. French, J. Arrizabalaga and A. Cunningham (Cambridge 1994), pp. 33–34.

5. "theoretical": "experiential" L שﬨ.

6. "change": "frequent change" L.

7. "individuals": Our translation follows the Hebrew *ishim*, whose intention seems to be the bodily constitutions and temperaments that vary significantly from individual to individual. The Latin took this as an alternative plural for *anashim*, i.e. people.

8. "force of the spheres": "forces of the spheres" L.

9. "much": "the cause" l.

10. "he will understand the effects of": "he will know how to prepare" L

11. "he will be able to make": "he will know and be able to make" L.

12. "as Hippocrates said": om. L.

13. Beginning of the first of Hippocrates' Aphorisms.

14. "but only [some of] its many parts"; cf. L: "but only with many efforts and dangers."

15. "and those of the latter generations are like a very fine needle": om. L.

16. "It . . . an uncommonly wondrous thing": om. L.

17. "as we have said": om. L.

18. "Sometimes they go to those who do have this knowledge or to those of whom they think that they have this knowledge and accordingly choose the times for their treatment": "Therefore doctors sometimes go to those whom they believe have some understanding in the knowledge of the stars, and they rule themselves (regulate what they do) by the statement or advice of those men, when choosing the time to do anything" L.

19. This sentence indicates that the chief utility of astrology lies in the determination of the proper times for administering treatment—rather than, say, determining the bodily dispositions and temperaments.

20. "and one of the experts in medicine in our time": om. L.

21. "since he thought something that is not so": an expression of modesty; i.e., he thought that I am an expert; "whom he thought to have some knowledge in the mentioned art" L.

22. "to compose a concise summary (*kelal qaṭan*) of astrology which a physician needs every day for the administration of purgatives, potions and vomitives, and bleedings": L translates: "to compose a concise treatise of those things which a physician needs every day for the administration of purgatives, potions and vomitives, and for bloodletting, since [knowledge] of astrology is necessary for such things".

23. "I . . . request": L translates: "And therefore, since I wanted to obey him, . . . I composed this small treatise".

24. This sentence is unclear in the original; the intention seems to be: the author fears that, were he to be overly modest, and refuse the request, it would harm the reputation that he has already established for himself.

25. "according to my ability": "according to my poor knowledge" L.

26. L adds: "without Whom nothing is achieved".

27. "concise summary (*kelal qaṭan*)": "treatise" L.

28. "who knows no theory at all": "who has no knowledge of the science of astrology" L.

29. "way": "with an almanac" add. L.

30. "something that could also be obtained from experts": "by means of those who know how to compute" L.

31. "the ways": "the two ways" L.

32. "in one of the ways mentioned": om. L.

33. "purgatives, bleedings and vomitives": "bleedings, purgatives, laxatives and vomitives" L.

34. "an astrologer or experienced astronomer": "someone" L.

35. A number of Arabic treatises deal with the question of what a physician ought to know in the field of astrology in order to treat a patient successfully. A typical example is *R. fi mā yaḥtāju al-ṭabīb min ʿilm al-falak* composed by ʿAdnān al-ʿAinzarbi, court physician of the Fatimid caliph aẓ-Ẓāfir bi-amr Allāh (ruled from 1149–1154); cf. M. Ullmann, *Die Medizin im Islam* (Handbuch der Orientalistik I, Ergänzungsband VI, 1) (Leiden/Köln, 1970), p. 255.

36. I.e. span on either side of the star within which it exerts its power by virtue of being in aspect, i.e. 6 degrees as in passages 23–24. Cf. Abraham Ibn Ezra, *Reshit Ḥokhmah*, end of the section of the planets: e.g. 8 degrees for Mars.

37. "attached to the almanac": om. L.

38. "<a quantity> less than 6°": "6 degrees or less" L. "4°").

39. "96° or 84°": "94°" or 86°").

40. "the harm caused by each planet is not as strong": "it is not as strong" L.

41. "in the house of": om. L.

42. "in the house of": om. L.

43. Ibn Ezra, *Sefer Reshit Ḥokhmah*, ed. Baqal, pp. VIII, English translation, p. 155.

44. "attached to the almanac": above-mentioned" L.

45. "known": "easily" add. L.

46. I.e., astrolabes; cf. Ibn aṣ-Ṣalt; Felix Klein-Franke, *Iatromathematics in Islam*, p. 103. Astrolabes have been found as part of the inventories of several physicians; cf. Antonio Contreras Mas, *Los médicos judíos en la Mallorca bajomedieval. Siglos XIV–XV* (Mallorca, 1997), p. 48.

47. The Hebrew is influenced by Latin syntax in this sentence here and in [30] below.

48. "which is called": "when it is" L.

49. "the": "this" L.

50. "attached to the almanac": om. L.

51. The astrological theory follows Abraham Ibn Ezra in places where he differs from Ptolemy. See e.g. *Tetrabiblos* I, 19 (ed. Loeb, p. 89), re "hypsōmata" (exaltations)—the note states that this has nothing to do with aphēlion. However, in Ibn Ezra's theory, the apogee does play a role; see *Reshit Ḥokhmah*, p. 107 (Baqal), and *Sefer ha-Ṭe'amim* [printed together with *Reshit Ḥokhmah*, Baqal, p. 107], where Ibn Ezra discusses an apparent difference of opinion between Ptolemy and the "sages of India" concerning the significance of a planet's being at or near apogee. Our author refers to both apogees (e.g. in [16] and in the tables) and to exaltations.

52. "beneficial influence": om. L.

53. "are": "sometimes somewhat" add. L.

54. See n. 47 above.

55. L adds: "that is [the signs] in which one season turns into another".

56. The Hebrew term *mamtin* for "slow" is also employed by Ibn Ezra, *Sefer ha-Me'orot*, ed. Baqal, p. 9.

57. Cf. Abū Ma'shar, *The Abbreviation of the Introduction to Astrology*, IV, 26–31 (ed. Ch. Burnett, K. Yamamoto and M. Yano (Leiden, 1994, p. 59); Ibn Ezra, *Sefer Reshit Ḥokhmah*, ed. Baqal, p. LIII, English translation, pp. 204–205.

58. "treatise": "The rules of this treatise": add. L.

59. "when it is <in conjunction> with Saturn or Mars": "when it is with Saturn or Mars in the same sign").

60. In Hebrew literally "the planet of the Sun"; cf. L: "Mercury".

61. "in one of the parts of the body": om. L.

62. "indicating": "dominating over" L.

63. Cf. pseudo-Ptolemy, *Fructus sive Centiloquium*, ed. E. Boer (Claudii Ptolemaei Opera quae exstant omnia III, 2) (Leipzig, 1961), no. 20; A. Chapman,

"Astrological medicine," *Health medicine and mortality in the sixteenth century*, Cambridge 1979, p.-296. For the correlation between the limbs of the body and their rulers, i.e., certain planets, and the theory of melothesia, i.e., zodiacal signs ruling over certain parts of the body, see Introduction.

64. "or to let blood from it": om. L.

65. "neck": "do not do this (i.e. surgery) nor let blood from the forearms when the Moon is in Gemini, which is the sign of the forearms" add. L.

66. Experience (*nissayon*, *tajriba*) and consensus (*haskamah*, *ijmā'*) are two epistemological standards which were very much in favor, especially in medicine and the occult sciences, though they are not valid criteria according to Aristotle and his followers. Concerning the first term, see Y.T. Langermann, "Maimonides' Repudiation of Astrology", *Maimonidean Studies*, edited by Arthur Hyman, vol.-2, (New York 1991): 123–158, pp. 135–139; concerning the second, see *idem*, "Science and the Cuzari", *Science in Context*, vol. 10, no. 3 (1997): 495–522, pp.-505–507.

67. "and it is accepted by the consensus of both the ancient and modern <authorities>": "and it has been verified empirically by the ancients, and the moderns . . . acquiesce" ⅃.

68. "authorities": "masters in astrology" L.

69. Cf. Chapman, ibid., p. 297.

70. "signs": "or hot and dry" add. L.

71. "And": "if you want to expel" add L.

72. "to perform bloodletting": "to evacuate the fine matter" L.

73. "i.e.,": "to purge" add. L.

74. "above the horizon", literally: "above the earth"; and so for the rest in these passages.

75. Cf. pseudo-Ptolemy, op. cit., no. 21.

76. "it indicates that it will purge more than necessary": "it indicates that it will not purge excessively and more than necessary" ⅃.

77. Cf. pseudo-Ptolemy, op. cit., no. 19: ἀμβλύνεται ἡ τοῦ καθαρσίου ἐνέργεια τῆς σελήνης συνοδευούσης τῷ Διί (The purgative power is blunted when the Moon makes a conjunction with Jupiter).

78. See *Sefer ha-Me'orot*, Baqal, p. 10, where Ibn Ezra does give this advice, but he mentions neither pseudo-Ptolemy nor the later astrologers.

79. "in Taurus": "like Taurus" ⅃.

80. "whatever patient it may be": om. L.

81. Translated after the Latin. The Hebrew reads: "that it is aspected by".

82. "potions and purgatives": "laxative potions" L.

83. "elections" (*mivḥarim*): times selected by means of astrological criteria.

84. "and methods": om. L.

85. L adds: "and even that is difficult".

86. "might be enough": "is enough" L.

87. "good": "very useful" L.

88. "For . . . possible": "For all this is necessary for the physician, or at least he should know about well-being" L.

89. "in a patient": translated after L; אוב: "because of diseases".

90. "the patient": cf. L.

91. Cf. pseudo-Ptolemy, op. cit., no. 57: ''Οτε ἴδης τὸν ἔβδομον τόπον καί τὸν κύριον αὐτοῦ κεκακωμένον ἐπὶ ἀρρώστου, ἄλλαξαι τὸν ἰατρόν (When you see that the seventh house or its Lord are harmed during an illness, change the physician).

92. "should for this reason be replaced": "should be replaced and another should be employed" L.

93. "who can understand mistakes?" (Psalms 19:13): om. L.

94. "should . . . honor": "should not make a mistake, and in this his honor is overturned" L.

95. "cause": "causes" L.

96. "what is correct and good": "what he ought <to do>" L.

97. Passages 53–54 are cited, word for word, as a note to Ibn Ezra, *Sefer ha-Me'orot*, ms Rav Qafih 36, f. 175a.

98. "alarmed": "confused" L.

99. I.e., astrologers; astrologi L.

100. "that the Moon is": om. L.

101. "configurations" (*temunot*). *Temunah* would seem to refer to the configuration of the astrological indicators.

102. L adds: "for when the wise man sees that the foolish man enjoys external support, he refrains from litigation until that support comes to an end".

103. I.e., its position at the beginning of the disease; cf. L.ב.

104. "crises": "i.e., critical days" add. L.

105. Cf. Hippocrates, *Aphorisms* II, 23.

106. David Ben Yom Tov refers here to the ancient hebdomadal theory (see Introduction).

107. I.e. after 28 days, when it returns to its initial position.

108. "a good crisis": i.e., that the disease resolves itself or, more simply, that the illness is over and the patient may recover.

109. I.e. the bodily stuff, e.g. excess or bad humors, which is the material cause of the malady.

110. "in a reinvigorated fashion": lit., as a convalescent.

111. "is also given": "is also given by the astrologers" L.

112. See Hippocrates, *Aphorisms* II,24. where the seventh and eleventh days are said to be indicative (*epidēlos*). In this and the following passages, David offers an astrological interpretation of Hippocrates' theory.

113. "reaches": "at another time" add. L.

114. See Ibn Ezra, *Sefer ha-Me'orot*, ed. Baqal, p. 9.

115. "after": "close to" L.

116. I.e. there is no medical cause that can be precisely determined.

117. "<can distinguish it>": Lב: "can distinguish critical day(s)".

118. The same general astrological principles used for the Moon in connection with acute diseases apply to the Sun in connection with chronic diseases, but the details are somewhat different. *Derekh,* "way", means here something like "general rule."

119. Cf. note L: "namely, of the attacks, for the seventh attack is critical in the case of a tertian and quartan fever, but in the case of a continuous fever the seventh day is critical".

120. "badness": "badness or harm" L.

121. "someone who does not practice this art": "the one who does not know" L.

122. "the day of the limit": "i.e. of the critical day" add. L.

123. Cf. *Sefer ha-Me'orot,* ed. Baqal, p. 12.

124. "according to the eclipse": "according to the kind of eclipse" L. Lunar eclipses are classified by magnitude, duration, and color; these items are listed in many medieval tables.

125. "the condition of": om. L.

126. "<of humors>"; cf. L.

127. I.e. a grave or ominous portent.

128. or: before opposition, cf. L: ante oppositum.

129. From "when it is slow" (passage 89) to the end of passage 90: a direct citation from Ibn Ezra, *Sefer ha-Me'orot,* Baqal, p. 14.

130. "the disease involves constipation": "the patient suffers from constipation" L.

131. "when the disease involves loose bowels": "when the patient suffers from loose bowels" L.

132. See *Sefer ha-Me'orot,* Baqal, p. 15.

133. *Sefer ha-Me'orot, loc. cit.,* displays the same information with regard to the trine and sextile aspects; otherwise, though, David and Ibn Ezra each conveys information not provided by the other.

134. "and man of understanding": om. L.

135. That is, those scientists—astrologers—whose art is based mainly upon "experience". See above, n. 13.

136. The nativity counterindicates—it suggests a different prognosis than do the astrological indicators associated with the illness.

137. On the reasons for failure in astrological prediction—cf. Ibn Ezra, *Sefer ha-Moladot,* Introduction, for a list of eight other reasons. The only overlap is the notion of divine intervention.

138. L adds: "who lives and reigns for ever and ever. Amen".

Glossary

Translation	David Judaeus	דוד בן יום טוב
(bodily) part	membrum	אבר 35,39
one of the parts of the body	-	אבר מן האברים 35
R. Abraham <ibn Ezra>	Rabi Abraam Aben Esdra	אברהם: ר׳ אברהם 46
yellow bile	colera	אדומה 38
a distinguished friend	notabilis amicus	אוהב: אחד מהאוהבים הנכבדים 8
		אויר ← מזלות
light	lumen, lux	אור 84,85,88,89
signs	signa	אותות 54
retrograde	retrogradans	אחורנית: שב אחורנית או נזור 27 ← שוב
it is slow in its motion	tardatur in suo cursu	אחר: יתאחר מהלכה 68
modern authorities	ultimi magistri	אחרונים 36
in the quality affected by it	in qualitate passiva	איכות: באיכות המתפעלת 61
in the quality active <in them>	in qualitate activa	באיכות פועלת 61
qualities	qualitates	איכויות 62,64
individuals	homines	אישים 3 ← טבעים
to administer a foodstuff	dare comestionem	אכל: האכיל 37
almanac	almanach, tabulae	אלמנאך 25,27
almanac	almanach, almenach, tabulae	אלמנך 11,16,21
		אמצעי ← מהלך
verification	verificatio	אמתה 76
most true	verior	אמתי: היותר אמתי 59
a common man	secularis	אנשים: אחד מאנשי ההמון 3
men of this science	astrologi	אנשי זאת החכמה 56
astrologer	-	אצטגנין 19
Leo	Leo	אריה 31,38
length	longitudo	אֹרֶךְ: אורך 88
earth (i.e. horizon)	terra	אֶרֶץ 42,43,47
		אש ← מזלות
to chose the times, the selection of the times	electio temporum	בחירה: בחירת העתים 7,19,49
crisis	boaran	בחראן 55,67,70,73,94 ← בכראן
crises	boaran	בחראנים 56,58,59,69 ← בחרנים
a day of crisis	dies boaran	בחראני 69
on a day on which a crisis does not fall	in die in quo non est boaran	יום שאינו בחראני 55
crises	dies cretici	בחרנים 3 ← בחראנים

Ptolemy	Tolomeus	בטלמיוס 45,52
house	domus	בית 25,30,78,79
houses	domus	בתים 16
good and complete crisis	boaran bonum et perfectum	בכראן: בכראן טוב ושלם 55 ← בחראן
Lord	dominus	בעל 27,42
man of understanding	-	לב - 93
experienced astronomer	-	נסיון בחכמת הכוכבים 19 -
opponent	adversarius	ריב 57 -
wise opponent	sapiens litigans	הריב המשכיל 57 -
a foolish opponent	stultus <litigans>	הריב השכל 57 -
Lord	dominus	בעלים 52
the masters of this science	scientes in hac scientia	בעלי זאת החכמה 20
expert	sciens	בקי 74
iron <instrument>	ferrum	ברזל 35
health	sanitas	בריאות 1,53 בשר ← רופא
Virgo	Virgo	בתולה 31,38
apogee	altitudo	גבהות 27,28,44,91
term, limit, crisis	terminus, terminus seu boaran	גבול 16,25,63,69,76, ← יום
a good crisis	terminus bonus sive boaran bonum	טוב - 64
crises	boaran, termini	גבולים 66,67,82
to overwhelm, strengthening, to overcome	conari super, habere conatum esse conatus, dominare super	גבר: התגבר (על) 57,64,70,72,76
Capricorn	Capricornus	גדי 31,38
body	corpus	גוף 21,84
<human> bodies	corpora	גופות 1 ← מזל גופים ← מזלות
orb, orbit, sphere	circulus	גלגל 27,44,72 גלגלים ← כח גלגלי ← כח,כחות, צורות
to be in conjunction with	habere coniunctionem	דבק 42
medical things	res medicinales	דברים: הדברים הרפואיים 2
Pisces	Piscis	דגים 31,38 דלוג ← קדחות
Aquarius	Aquarius	דלי 31,38 דם ← נקז, ריק
the <correct> ways to treat	vie medicine	דרכים: דרכי הרפואה 54 ← התחלות
to be derived from	capitur super hoc demonstratio	הוראה: ילקח הוראה עליו 76
indications	demonstrationes	הוראות 94
astrologer	astrologus	הובר 2
harm	(ש חזק =) fortis	הזק 24
recognizing	cognoscere	הכרה 54 הליכה ← ממתין המון ← אנשים

treatment	regimen	הנהגה 51
contrariness	contrarietas	הפכות 61
contrariness	contrarietas	הפכיות 64
vomitives	vomitiva	הקאות 19
prognosis	prenosticatio, prenosticare	הקדמה: הקדמת הידיעה 51,76
		הקזה ← ריק
bleedings	flebotomie	הקזות 8,19,49
cycles(?)	revolutiones	הקפים 75
logical reasoning	ratio	הקש 55
so also	considera	וההקש על זה 24 (= והקש על זה ש)
practice	uti	הרגל 14
		הרכבה ← עולם
to give a purgative	purgatio vel evacuatio	הרקה 37,42
the beginning of the disease	principium egritudinis	התחלה: התחלת החולי 62,63 ← תחלה
the principles and fundamentals of this science	principia scientie	התחלות: התחלות החכמה ושרשיה 50
the principles and methods of this science	principia scientie	- החכמה ודרכיה 50
relationship	proportio	התיחסות 1
		זנב ← תלי
since the Sun rose	ab ortu Solis	זריחה: מעת הזריחה 26
malefic conjunction or aspect	coniunctio vel aspectus dampnosus	חבור: חבור או מבט מזיק 52
surgery	incisio vel apertio	חבורה 35,36
to form a conjunction	coniungi, habere coniunctionem	חבר: התחבר 25,78,87
		חד ← עלה
patient	infirmus, eger	חולה 51–53,80,83,49
		חזק ← מבטים
<human> life	vita hominis	חיים 4
learned	-	חכם 46
scholar	sciens	חכמים: אחד מן החכמים 3 ← משפט
experienced scholars	experimentatores	חכמי הנסיון 93
the learned physicians	auctores medicine	חכמי הרפואה 55
science	scientia	חכמה 6,49,51,74,94, ← אנשים, בעלים, התחלות, ספרים
astrology	scientia stellarum	חכמת הכוכבים 1,6,8 ← בעל
illness, disease	egritudo, infirmitas, eger	חלי: חולי 1,54,60,64,65,70,79, תחלה, 84,86–88,90,91 ← התחלה
as a convalescent	sicut ille qui recuperat virtutem	חלף: כמי שיחליף כח 65
part	pars	חלק 1
theoretical part	pars experimentalis	החלק: החלק העיוני 1
parts, subdisciplines	labores et pericula, particulae	חלקים 4
Sun	Sol	חמה 13,29,34,48
matter	materia	חׁמר: חומר 64
the matter moved by it	-	החומר המתנועע בו 57
decrease	diminutio	חסרון 85

to compute	computare	חשב 11
computation	compotum	חשבון 14, → ידיעה
Nature	natura	טבע 57,65,70,72
the <different> natures of individuals	natura hominum	טבעים: טבעי האישים 2
benefic, beneficial, good	bonus	טוב 29,58,59,76,78,80,83,87,92 → גבול, כוכבים
beneficial influence	-	טובה 29
Aries	Aries	טלה 31,36,38,60,61,82
mistake	errare	טעות 54
an error or mistake	error	ושבוש 52 -
knowledge, to learn	scire, computare, scientia	ידיעה 2,3,12,13,50,51,77 → הקדמה, קדם
the study of computation	computare	ידיעת החשבון 14
experts	illos qui id computare sciunt	יודעים: היודעים בזה 15
day	dies	יום 59,62,63,66,73 → בחראני, שעות
a day of a crisis	dies creticus, dies termini (i.e. dies creticus)	הגבול 66,80 -
days	dies, dies cretice	ימים 15,55,66,67,69,70,75, 92
descending	descendere	יורד 27,44
ratio	<pro>portio	יחס 75
		יסודות → עולם
to excerpt	abstrahere	יצא: הוציא 16
Moon	luna	ירח 67,47,27,17,56,06–65,93
declining	in declinatione	ירידה: בירידה 64
to become chronic	antiquatio	ישן: התישן 70 יָשֵׁן → עלות
cardines	caville	יתדות 82
exaltation	honor	כבוד 16,25,53,78
planet, Mercury	Mercurius, planeta	כוכב 13,22,24,25,27,29,30,32,34, 41,42,46,47,78,80,87
retrograde planet	planeta retrogradans	שהוא שב אחורנית 43 -
It is said that one planet is in conjunction with another	Dicitur enim quod una stella est cum alia	יאמר שהכוכב עם כוכב אחר 21
planets	planete, stelle	כוכבים 11,13,15,16,21,42,43,59 → חכמה, מקומות
good or benefic planets	planete boni vel benefortunati	הכוכבים: הכוכבים הטובים או המצליחים 29
one of the benefics	aliquis bonus planeta	אחד מן הכוכבים הטובים 48
to determine, take care	pervenire, facere, respicere	כון: כוון/כוין 26,41,42,46
strength	virtus	כח 21,23,25,29,42,43,45,47, 64 → חלף
the force of the spheres	virtutes celestes	הגלגלים 2 -
dodecatemorion	virtus .xii.	י"ב 33 -
the force of the spheres	virtus celestis	הכח: הכח הגלגליי 1
the forces of the spheres	virtutes celestes	כחות: הכחות הגלגליות 3
instruments	instrumenta	כלים 26
a concise summary	tractatus parvus	כלל: כלל קטן 8
this concise summary	huiusmodi tractatus	הכלל: זה הכלל הקטן 11

heart	-	בעל → 5 לב
hearts	corda	לבבות 5
Moon	Luna	לבנה 14,29,32,33-38,40,42, 44-48,63,67,78,80-84,86,88,92
tables	tabule, sistrenus	לוחות 17,18,21,25-27,33
		קונדריס →
humor, fluid	humor	ליחה 37,40,86
phlegm	fleuma	הליחה: הליחה הלבנה 38
Mars	Mars	מאדים 13,29,33,34
Libra	Libra	מאזנים 31,33,38,61,82
elections	electiones	מבחרים 50
aspect	aspectus	מבט 23,33,48,72,76,80,87,92
		חבור →
opposition	aspectus oppositi, aspectus oppositus vel oppositio	נכח - 22,63
the aspect of an opposition or quartile	aspectus oppositus vel quadratus	נכח או מרובע 92 -
quartile aspect, the aspect of a quartile	aspectus quarti (quartus)	רביעית - 22,24,34,63,71
bad aspect	malus aspectus	רע - 43
trine, the aspect of a trine	aspectus tertii, aspectus tertius	שלישית - 22,34,66,92
exact aspect	aspectus completus	שלם - 24
sextile, the aspect of a sextile	aspectus sexti, aspectus .vi., aspectus sextus	ששית - 22,34,66,92
aspects	aspectus	מבטים, 23,24,48,59,64 72,76 ← תקיף
strong aspects	aspectus fortes	המבטים: המבטים החזקים 71
complicated	turbatus	מְבֻלְבָּל: מבולבל 14
fast	velox	מהיר 32,67,89
quickness	properatio	מהירות 83
motion	vadere, cursus	מהלך 32,67 ← אחר, מתן, ממתין
its mean motion, the mean [daily] motion	(suus motus) medius, cursus medius	מהלכו האמצעי 32
natal horoscope	nativitas	מולד 94
		מומחים ← רופאים
malefic	dampnosus, planeta dampnosus	מזיק, 29,52,76 ← חבור
malefics	mali planete et dampnosi, planete mali seu dampnosi, planete mali, planete dampnosi	מזיקים 29,33,72,76
one of the malefics	planeta dampnosus	אחד מן המזיקים 43
sign	signum	מזל 21,26,30,33-37,39,41,47,48 86,87
tropical sign	signum mobile	מתהפך 83 -
fixed sign	signum stabile	עומד 83 -
bicorporal sign	signum medium	שני גופות 83 -
the sign rising	signum quod ascendit	המזל: המזל העולה 26
the rising sign	signum ascendentis, signum ascendens	הצומח - 27,30,82
signs		

\<one of\> the fiery signs	signa	מזלות 16,38
\<one of\> the watery signs	signum igneum	האש 38 -
\<one of\> the earthy signs	signum aque	המים 38 -
tropical signs	signum terrestre	העפר 38 -
	signa convertibilia seu mobilia	מתהפכים 13 -
fixed signs	signa stabilia	עומדים 13 -
bicorporal signs	signa media seu duorum corporum	שני גופים 13 -
one of the airy signs	aliquod signum aeris	אחד ממזלות האויר 38
one of the watery signs	unum signorum aque, aliquod signum aque	אחד ממזלות המים 40,48
in the east	in orientem	מזרח: בפאת המזרח 26
conjunction	coniunctio	מחברת 33,87,88
		מחובר ← ספרים
a very fine needle	-	מחט: מחט סדקית 5
kind	-	מין 1
-	-	מינים: מיני השנוי 1
art, execution	ars, medicina, opera	מלאכה 3,6,8
someone who does not practice this art	nesciens	מי שאינו בעל זאת המלאכה 77
(the art of) medicine	practica (scientie) medicine,	מלאכת הרפואה 1,2
arts, subdisciplines	ars medicine	
slow in motion	artes	מלאכות 1,4
	tardus in suo motu vel cursu	ממתין: ממתין בהליכתו 32
slow in its motion	tardus in suo cursu	ממתנת בהליכתה 33
slow in its motion	tardus in suo cursu	ממתנת במהלכה 67
tested \<by experience\>	experimentatus	מְנֻסֶּה: מנוסה 36
accepted by the consensus	probatus	מֻסְכָּם: מוסכם 36
number		
degree	numerus	מספר 75
degrees	gradus	מעלה 26-28,33
position	gradus	מעלות 22–24,28,32,33,41
	status vel situs	מצב 72
benefics		מצליח ← כוכבים
position	planete boni	מצליחים 72
	locus	מקום 56–63,65–68,70–72,78, 81,91
positions	loca, locus	מקומות 11,13,15,76
the positions of the planets	loca planetarum, planetarum loca	הכוכבים 18,19 -
vomitives	vomitiva	מקיאים 8
quartile \<aspect\>	quadratum, quartus	מרובע 62,78,81,82 ← מבט
bath	balneum	מרחץ 48
purgative		משכיל ← בעל, רופא
	purga vel laxativum, potatio laxativa, laxativum	משלשל 44,45
purgatives	laxativa	משלשלים 8,19 ← משקים
judgement	iudicare	משפט 87
astrologers	sapientes in iudicio	חכמי המשפט 16
		משקה ← קיא, שלשל

emetic	potatio vomitativa	להקיא 47 -
potions	ciropes	משקים 8
potions and purgatives	potationes laxative	המשקים: המשקים והמשלשלים 49
		מתהפך ← מזל, מזלות
it is slow in its motion	est tardus in suo cursu	מתן: ימתין במהלכו 89
certain	firmus	נאמן 82
to form an aspect, to aspect	inspicere, aspicere, habere aspectum	נבט: הביט 25,44,46,78,80,87
Venus	Venus	נגה 13
		נוע: מתנועע ← חמר
to make a move, to move	se movere, moveri	התנועע 57,65
harmed	impeditus	נזוק 52
retrograde	retrogradans, retrogradus	נזור 27,90 ← אחורנית
to be harmful	nocere, dampnificare	נזק: הזיק 43,76,89
to be harmed	esse dampnificatus	הוזק 52
		נכבד ← אוהב
proper	firmus	נכון 58
opposition, the aspect of an opposition	oppositum	נכח 33,34,48,59–61,71,78,81, 82,90 ← מבט
experience	experimentum	נסיון, 55 ← בעל, חכמים
overcome	devictus	נצוח 57
to overcome, win	vitare, vincere	נצח: ניצח 65,72
to be defeated	vinci	נוצח 72
to be eclipsed	eclipsari	נקדר: היה נקדר 33
to let blood		נקז: הקיז 36 ← ריק
to let blood, to bleed	flebotomari vel febotomiam (*sic*) facere, sanguines minuere	הקיז דם 34,39
cause, reason	cause, ratio	סבה 54–56,66,69,84,
		סדקית ← מחט
end	finis	סוף 33,67
sign	signum	סמן: סימן 78,81,87,92
books	libri	ספרים 49
the books composed on this subject	libri de hoc compilati	הספרים: הספרים המחוברים בזה 10
the books on this science	libri scientie astrologie	ספרי החכמה 16
Cancer	Carcer (*sic*), Cancer	סרטן 31,38
rising	ascendens	עולה 27,28,44 ← מזל
the world of composite things	hoc seculum	עולם: עולם ההרכבה 1
the world of the elements	mundus elementorum	היסודות 1 -
		עומד ← מזל, מזלות
to awaken, become active	moveri	עור: התעורר 57,71,72
someone who knows no theory at all	nil sciens	עיון: מי שאין לו מאומה מן העיון 12
careful consideration	respectus magnus et deliberatio	גדול 8 -
		עיוני ← חלק

to study	tractare de	עיין 1
disease	infirmitas, egritudo	עלה 57,76 ← תחלה
diseases	egri	עלות 52
acute diseases	egritudines acute	העלות: העלות החדות 74
chronic diseases	egritudines antiquate	- הישנות 74
patient	infirmus	עלול 48
		עפר ← מזלות
constipation	constipatus	עצור 91
Scorpio	Scorpius	עקרב 31,33,38,41
		עת ← זריחה
proper and improper times	tempora perfecta et inutilia	עתים: עתים נכונים ובלתי נאותים 50 ← בחירה
times	tempora	עתות 94
		פאה ← מזרח
		פועל ← איכות
agents	agentes	פועלים 2 ← פעולה
the distant and proximate agents	agentia procul et prope	הפועלים: הפועלים הרחוקים והקרובים 3
decan	facies	פנים 16,25
those who are passive, passive things	patientes	פעל: המתפעלים 2,3
		מתפעל ← איכות
effect	operatio, opera	פעולה 45
the effect of the agents	operatio agentium	פעולת הפועלים 2
to separate from	recedere ab	פרד: התפרד מן 33
ways	casus	צדדים 1
Jupiter	Iuppiter, Iupiter	צדק 13,29,45,92
right	iustus	צודק: צודקים 58
most right	iustior	היותר צודק 59
neck	collum	צואר 36
Ascendant	ascendens	צומח 26,27,42,52, מזל ←
forms	vultus	צורות 1
the forms of the spheres	vultus celestes	הצורות הגלגליות 1
continuous fevers	febres continue	קדחות: קדחות תמידיות 75
intermittent fevers	febres que veniunt saltando	הקדחות: הקדחות הבאות בדלוג 75
to appear earlier	anticipari	קדם 67
to make a prognosis	prenoscitare	הקדים הידיעה 3
to be eclipsed	eclipsari	קדר: נקדר 33,81
eclipse	eclipsis	קדרות 81
the astronomical tables	sistrenum (?) tabularum	קונדריס: קונדריס הלוחות 16,17
regurgitate	vomitare purgam	קיא: הקיא המשקה 42,43 ← משקה
shame	verecundia	קלון 16
in a concise way	per modum abbreviationis	קצור: דרך קצור 16
difficult	difficilis	קשה 14
Sagittarius	Sagittarius	קשת 31,38

head, beginning	caput	תלי → 36,60,68,82 ראש
minutes, ancient authorities	minuta, primi magistri	ראשונים 32,36
		רביעי → מבט
apogee	altitudo	רום 16
physician	medicus	רופא 3,6,8,51–53,95
the healer of all flesh	medicus omnis carnis	כל בשר 94 -
learned physician	medicus sciens	משכיל 93 -
physicians	medici	רופאים 70
expert physicians	sollemnes medici	מומחים 55 -
		ריב → בעל
to expel	purgare vel evacuare, purgare	ריק: להריק 37,38,40
to expel blood, i.e., to perform bloodletting	flebotomare vel materiam subtilem evacuare	להריק הדם כלומר להקיזה 38
to expel in general	facere evacuationem generalem —id est purgare	להריק הליחה הקזה כוללת 40
bad(ness), evil	malus, malum	רע 59,76,80,81,83,88,89,91
corruption, evil	mala, malum	רעה 33,91
corruptions	mala vel impedimenta	רעות 29
to be cured	sanatus esse	רפא: התרפא 90
medicine	scientia, medicina, scientia medicine	רפואה 8,51,55,73 → דרכים, חכמים, מלאכה
to purge	laxativa	לשלשל 37 -
		רפואי → דבר
impression	signum	רשֶׁם: רושם 1
to be faulty	errare	שבוש 53 → טעות
the seventh \<house\>	septimum	שביעי: השביעי 52
Saturn	Saturnus	שבתאי 13,29,32–34,44,88, 89,91
mistakes	errata	שגיאות 53
to be retrograde	esse retrogradans	שוב: שב אחורנית 43,47
Taurus	Taurus	שור 31,36,38,47
black bile	malencolia	שחורה 38
triplicity	triplicitas	שלישות 16,25
		שלישית → מבט
		שלם → מבט
perfection, completeness	perfectio	שלמות 2,3,76
purging, loose bowels	evacuatio, laxus	שלשול 44,91
		שלשל → רפואה
that the purgative will not purge	quod purga non faciet operationem	כי לא ישלשל המשקה 44
application	servire	שמוש 3
Sun	Sol	שמש 26,33,74,79,90
hatred (detriment)	malivolentia, malivolus	שנאה 16,30,79
change	transmutatio	שנוי → 1 מינים
years	anni	שנים 15
hour	hora	שעה 26
hours	hore	שעות 26
the hours of the day	hore diei	היום 26 -
perigee	profunditas, descensus sive	שפלות 16,28,79,91

to administer (a potion)	bisextus, dedecus, descensus dare potationem, dare ad bibendum, dare	שקה: השקה 37,44,45
principles	radices	שרשים 50,94
		ששית ← מבט
overlap	societas	שתוף 1
Gemini	Geminis (*sic*)	תאומים 31,34,38
nature	natura	תולדה 80
increase	multiplicatio, augmentum	תוספת 84,89
the beginning of a disease	principium egritudinis	תחלה: תחלת החולי 56–58,60,63, 65,66,70,72,78,80-83,86 ← התחלה
the beginning of a disease	principium egritudinis	תחלת העלה 57
completeness	finis	תכלית 4
the Head or Tail of the nodes	caput draconis vel cauda eius	תלי: ראש התלי או זנבו 33
configuration	figura	תמונה 58
configurations	dispositiones	תמונות 56
		תמידי ← קדחות
stipulations	condiciones	תנאים 74
movement	motus	תנועה 1
the strongest (aspect)	fortior aspectus	תקיף: התקיף שבמבטים 59

Bibliography

Abū Ma'shar, *The Abbreviation of the Introduction to Astrology*, ed. Ch. Burnett, K. Yamamoto and M. Yano (Leiden, 1994).

'Alī b. Rabban al-Ṭabarī, *Firdaws al-ḥikma*, ed. M.Z. Siddiqi (Berlin, 1928).

Baqal, Meir (ed.), *Sefer Mishpaṭei ha-Kokhavim* (a collection of Ibn Ezra's astrological treatises) (Jerusalem, 1971).

Barton, Tamsyn S., *Power and Knowledge: Astrology, Physiognomics, and Medicine under the Roman Empire* (Ann Arbor, 1994).

al-Bīrūnī, *K. al-Tafhīm*, (*The Book of Instruction in the Elements of Astrology*, translated by R. Ramsay Wright (London, 1934).

Bos, Gerrit, "R. Moshe Narboni, Philosopher and physician," *Medieval Encounters*, vol. 1, no. 2 (1995): 219–251.

Bos, G., and C. Burnett, *Scientific Weather Forecasting in the Middle Ages* (London, 2000).

Celsus, *De medicina*, with an English translation by W.G. Spencer (Loeb Classical Library), vol. 1 (Cambridge and London, 1935, repr. 1971).

Chapman, Allan, "Astrological medicine," *Health, medicine and mortality in the sixteenth century*, ed. by Charles Webster (Cambridge 1979), 275–300.

José Chabás, *L'Astronomia de Jacob ben David Bonjorn* (Barcelona, 1992).

Encyclopaedia Judaica, 16 vols. Jerusalem 1971.

Contreras Mas, Antonio, *Los médicos judíos en la Mallorca bajomedieval. Siglos XIV–XV* (Mallorca, 1997).

French, R., "Astrology in medical practice," *Practical medicine from Salerno to the Black Death*, ed. L. García-Ballester, R. French, J. Arrizabalaga & A. Cunningham (Cambridge 1994), pp. 30–59.

Galen, *On Regimen in Acute Diseases*; see M. Lyons, Galen, *On the Parts of Medicine* . . .

Galen, *On Antecedent Causes,* edited with an introduction, translation and commentary by R.J. Hankinson (Cambridge, 1998).

Geller, M.J., "Akkadian Healing Therapies in the Babylonian Talmud," *Max-Planck Institut fur Wissenschaftsgeschichte,* preprint 259 (2004).

Goldstein, Bernard, "Descriptions of Astronomical Instruments in Hebrew," in David A. King and George Saliba (eds.), *From Deferent to Equant: A Volume of Studies in History of Science in the Ancient and Medieval Near East in Honor of E.S. Kennedy* (New York, 1987), pp. 105–141.

Grmek, Mirko D., *Diseases in the Ancient Greek World* (translated from the French by Mireille Muellner and Leonard Muellner, Baltimore and London, 1989).

Gross, H., *Gallia Judaica, Dictionnaire géographique de la France d'après les sources Rabbiniques* (Paris, 1897).

Guthrie, W.K.C., *A History of Greek Philosophy,* vol. 1, *The earlier Presocratics and the Pythagoreans* (Cambridge, 1962).

Harvey, Steven (ed.), *The Medieval Hebrew Encyclopedias of Science and Philosophy* (Dordrecht, 2000).

Hephaestios Thebanus Apotelesmatica, ed. David Pingree, 2 (Leipzig, 1983).

Hippocrates, *Prognostica,* ed. H. Kuehlwein, *Hippocratis opera,* I (Leipzig, 1884).

Idem, *Airs Waters, Places*: Hippocrates, with an English translation by W.H.S. Jones, vol. 1 (Loeb Classical Library) (Cambridge, USA, and London, 1923, repr. 1984).

Idem, *Aphorisms*: Hippocrates, with an English translation by W.H.S. Jones, vol. 4 (Loeb Classical Library) (Cambridge, USA, and London, 1931, repr. 1979).

Idem, *On Fleshes*: Hippocrates, vol. VIII, edited and translated by Paul Potter (Loeb Classical Library) (Cambridge and London, 1995).

Holford-Strevens, Leofranc, "The Harmonious Pulse," *Classical Quarterly* 43 (1999): 475–497.

Huizenga, E., "Die conste vanden almenack," *Queeste* 1 (1994): 12–33.

Ibn Ezra, Abraham, *Sefer Reshit Ḥokhmah,* and *Sefer ha-Ṭe' amim,* ed. by M. Baqal (Jerusalem, 1973).

Idem, *Sefer ha-Me'orot*: see *Sefer Mishpatei ha-Kokhavim.*

Idem, *Sefer ha-Moladot,* in: *Seder 12 ha-Moladot,* ed. by M. Baqal, (Jerusalem, 1995): 193–248.

Idem, *Sefer Mishpaṭei ha-Kokhavim, Sefer ha-Me'orot,* ed. Meir Baqal, (Jerusalem, 1971).

Idem: See as well Baqal, Meir; Levy, Raphael.

Ibn Rushd, *K. al-Kulliyyāt* (Algiers, 1989).

Isaacs, Haskell, "Arabic medical literature," in M.J.L. Young, J.D. Latham, and R.B. Serjeant, *Religion, Learning, and Science in the 'Abbasid*

Period (Cambridge, 1990).

Idem, *Medical and Para-Medical Manuscripts in Cambridge Genizah Collections* (Cambridge, 1994).

Jacquart, Danielle, "Bernard de Gordon et l'astrologie," *Centaurus* 45 (2003) [Bernard R. Goldstein Festschrift]: 151–158.

Kayserling, M., *Geschichte der Juden in Portugal* (Leipzig, 1867).

Klein-Franke, F., *Iatromathematics in Islam* (Hildesheim, 1984).

Langermann, Y. Tzvi, "Maimonides' Repudiation of Astrology," *Maimonidean Studies* 2 (1991): 123–158.

Idem, *The Jews and the Sciences in the Middle Ages* (Aldershot, 1999).

Idem, "Gersonides on Astrology," appended to Levi ben Gershom, *The Wars of the Lord*, translated by Seymour Feldman, vol. 3 (Philadelphia and New York, 1999).

Idem, "Hebrew Astronomy: Deep Soundings from a Rich Tradition," in Helaine Selin (ed.), *Astronomy Across Cultures* (Dordrecht, 2000), pp. 555–584.

Idem, "Cosmology and Cosmogony in *Doresh Reshumoth*, a Thirteenth-Century Commentary on the Torah," *Harvard Theological Review* 97 (2004): 199–227.

Lemay, Richard, "Origin and Success of the *Kitab Thamara* of Abū Ja'far ibn Yusuf," *Proceedings of the First International Symposium for the History of Arabic Science* (Aleppo, 1978).

Levy, Raphael, *The Astrological Works of Abraham ibn Ezra* (Baltimore, 1927).

Levy, Raphael and Francisco Cantera, *The Beginning of Wisdom. An Astrological Treatise by Abraham Ibn Ezra* (Baltimore, 1939).

Lloyd, G.E.R., *The Revolutions of Wisdom: Studies in the Claims and Practice of Ancient Greek Science* (Berkeley, 1987).

Lyons, M., Galen, *On the Parts of Medicine, On Cohesive Causes, On Regimen in Acute Diseases in accordance with the Theories of Hippocrates* (Berlin, 1969).

Neubauer, Ad., *Catalogue of the Hebrew Manuscripts in the Bodleian Library* (Oxford 1886, repr. 1994). And: *Supplement of Addenda and Corrigenda* compiled under the direction of Malachi Beit-Arié and edited by R.A. May (Oxford 1994).

Nutton, Vivian, Galen, *De Praecognitione, Corpus Medicorum Graecorum* 5.8.1 (Berlin, 1979).

Pines, S., "The Semantic Distinction between the terms *Astronomy* and *Astrology* according to Al-Biruni," *Isis* 53 (1964), 343–349; repr., *The Collected Works of Shlomo Pines*, vol. 2 (Jerusalem and Leiden, 1986).

Pseudo-Ptolemy, *Fructus sive Centiloquium*, ed. E. Boer (Claudii Ptolemaei Opera quae exstant omnia III, 2) (Leipzig, 1961).

Ptolemy, *Tetrabiblos*, edited and translated by F.E. Robbins (Loeb

Classical Library) (Cambridge, USA, and London, 1940, repr. 1994).

Richler, Benjamin, *Hebrew Manuscripts in the Biblioteca Palatina in Parma* (Jerusalem, 2001) (Cambridge, USA, and London, 1971).

Rinaldi, Michele, "Pontano, Tapezunzio ed il Graecus Interpres del Centiloquio pseudo-tolemico," *Atti della Accademia Pontaniana*, N.S. 48, anno accademico 1999 (Napoli, 2000): 127–171.

Roscher, W.H., *Die hippokratische Schrift von der Siebenzahl in ihrer vierfachen Ueberlieferung* (Paderborn, 1913).

Sambursky, S. and S. Pines, *The Concept of Time in Late Neoplatonism* (Jerusalem, 1987).

Sezgin, Fuat, *Geschichte des arabischen Schrifttums*. Band III: Medizin-Pharmazie-Zoologie-Tierheilkunde bis ca. 430 H. (Leiden, 1970).

Idem, *Geschichte des arabischen Schrifttums*, vol. VII: Astrologie-Meteorologie und Verwandtes, Bis ca. 430 H (Leiden, 1979).

Shatzmiller, Joseph, "In search of the "Book of Figures": Medicine and astrology in Montpellier at the turn of the fourteenth century," *AJS Review*, volume 7–8 (1982–1983): 383–407.

Singer, P.J., "Levels of Explanation in Galen," *Classical Quarterly* 47 (1997): 525–542.

Idem, *Galen: Selected Works* (Oxford, 1997).

Steinschneider, M., *Catalogus Librorum Hebraeorum in Bibliotheca Bodleiana* (Berlin, 1852–1860, repr. Hildesheim 1964).

Idem, "Yusuf ben Ibrahim und Ahmed ibn Yusuf," *Bibliotheca Mathematica*, new series 2 (1888), 49–117.

Idem, *Die hebräischen Übersetzungen des Mittelalters und die Juden als Dolmetscher* (Berlin, 1893, repr. Graz 1956).

Theology of Arithmetic, The, translated by Robin Waterfield (Grand Rapids, 1988).

Thorndike, L., 'The Latin Translations of the Astrological Tracts of Abraham Avenezra,' *Isis*, 35, 1944: 293–302.

Ullmann, M., *Die Medizin im Islam* (Handbuch der Orientalistik I, Ergänzungsband VI, 1) (Leiden/Köln, 1970).

Zotenberg, H. (ed.), *Catalogues des Manuscrits Hébreux et Samaritains de la Bibliothèque Impériale* (Paris, 1866).

Index

ability, 10
Abraham <Ibn Ezra>, 46
action. *See* aspect
    of a wise opponent compared to that of a foolish one, 57
administration, 8
agents. *See* effect
almanac, 11, 16, 26. *See also* tables
apogee, 16. *See also* degree, planet, position, Saturn
    the orbit of its, 44
application, 3
Aquarius, 31, 38
Aries, 31, 36, 38. *See also* beginning, opposite
art, 3, 6, 77
    the art of medicine, 2
arts, 1, 4, 5
Ascendant, 26, 52. *See* Lord
aspect, 23–25, 33, 48, 52, 72, 78, 80, 87. *See also* degree
    of the action of causes, 3
    of the disposition of passive bodies, 3
    quartile, 22, 63
    of a quartile or opposition, 34, 71
    of a trine or sextile, 34
    bad, 43
    of a sextile, 66
    of a trine, 66
    of the malefic, 76
    of an opposition, 78
    a sextile or trine, 92
    of an opposition or quartile, 92

www.ingramcontent.com/pod-product-compliance
Lightning Source LLC
Chambersburg PA
CBHW080920100426
42812CB00007B/2330